D0122605

TRIBES

BESTSELLING BOOKS BY SETH GODIN

Meatball Sundae
The Dip
Small Is the New Big
All Marketers Are Liars
Free Prize Inside!
Purple Cow
The Big Red Fez
Survival Is Not Enough
Unleashing the Ideavirus
Permission Marketing

AND CHECK OUT THESE FREE E-BOOKS (GOOGLE 'EM):

Knock Knock
Who's There
Everyone's an Expert
The Bookstrapper's Bible

There are more than two thousand free articles by Seth on his blog. Visit www.SethGodin.com for more information . . . click on Seth's head to read them and join the tribe.

TRIBES

WE NEED *YOU* TO LEAD US

Seth Godin

PORTFOLIO

PORTFOLIO

Published by the Penguin Group

Penguin Group (USA) Inc., 375 Hudson Street, New York, New York 10014,
U.S.A. • Penguin Group (Canada), 90 Eglinton Avenue East, Suite 700, Toronto,
Ontario, Canada M4P 2Y3 (a division of Pearson Penguin Canada Inc.) • Pen-
guin Books Ltd, 80 Strand, London WC2R 0RL, England • Penguin Ireland,
25 St. Stephen's Green, Dublin 2, Ireland (a division of Penguin Books Ltd) • Pen-
guin Books Australia Ltd, 250 Camberwell Road, Camberwell, Victoria 3124,
Australia (a division of Pearson Australia Group Pty Ltd) • Penguin Books India
Pvt Ltd, 11 Community Centre, Panchsheel Park, New Delhi – 110 017, India
• Penguin Group (NZ), 67 Apollo Drive, Rosedale, North Shore 0632, New Zealand (a division of Pearson New Zealand Ltd.) • Penguin Books (South Africa)
(Pty) Ltd, 24 Sturdee Avenue, Rosebank, Johannesburg 2196, South Africa

Penguin Books Ltd, Registered Offices:
80 Strand, London WC2R 0RL, England

First published in 2008 by Portfolio,
a member of Penguin Group (USA) Inc.

15   17   19   21   22   20   18   16   14

LIBRARY OF CONGRESS CATALOGING IN PUBLICATION DATA
Godin, Seth.
Tribes : we need *you* to lead us / Seth Godin.
p.   cm.
ISBN: 978-1-59184-233-0
1. Leadership.   I. Title.
HD57.7.G6546 2008
658.4'092—dc22   2008024978

Printed in the United States of America
Set in Janson Text with Berthold Akzidenz Grotesk
Designed by Daniel Lagin

For Mo and Alex
Who want to change things—

and for the people who will be
lucky enough to join their tribe

TRIBES

JOEL SPOLSKY IS CHANGING THE WORLD.

Maybe not your world, but the world of programmers and software companies and the people who work with them. The *way* Joel is changing the world, though, is something every single one of us needs to pay attention to.

While Joel runs a small software company in New York City, his real passion is talking about *how* to run a small software company. Through blogs and books and conferences, Joel has changed the way many smart people think about finding, hiring, and managing programmers. Along the way, Joel has assembled a large and influential tribe of people who look to him for leadership.

A tribe is a group of people connected to one another, connected to a leader, and connected to an idea. For millions of years, human beings have been part of one tribe or another. A group needs only two things to be a tribe: a shared interest and a way to communicate. Joel provides both. He runs a profitable job board that attracts the very best programmers (and the best jobs) in the world. He even created the widely used Joel Test, which is a measure of how programmer friendly a job might be. A Google search on "Joel" returns seventy-six million matches, and Joel Spolsky is first, right where he belongs.

Tribes need leadership. Sometimes one person leads, sometimes more. People want connection and growth and something new. They want change. Joel's leadership provided change. He's given this tribe a lever to dramatically alter the way business is done in their industry. Along the way, he's found his passion (and grown his company).

You can't have a tribe without a leader—and you can't be a leader without a tribe.

Long, Strange Trip

Forty years ago, Jerry Garcia and the Grateful Dead made some decisions that changed the music industry forever. You might not be in the music business and you may never have been to a Dead concert, but the impact the Dead made affects almost every industry, including yours.

In addition to grossing more than $100 million during their career, the Dead helped us understand how tribes work.

They didn't succeed by selling records (they only had one Top 40 album). Instead, they succeeded by attracting and leading a tribe.

Human beings can't help it: we need to belong. One of the most powerful of our survival mechanisms is to be part of a tribe, to contribute to (and take from) a group of like-minded people. We are drawn to leaders and to their ideas, and we can't resist the rush of belonging and the thrill of the new.

When one Deadhead says to another, "2-14-70," it's like a secret code. The smiles and the hugs and handshakes define who we are—being in a tribe is a big part of how we see ourselves.

We want to belong not to just one tribe, it turns out, but to many. And if you give us tools and make it easy, we'll keep joining.

Tribes make our lives better. And leading a tribe is the best life of all.

Tribes Used to Be Local

Jacqueline Novogratz is changing the world. Not by leading everyone in her town, but by challenging people in twenty countries to join a movement. One at a time, Jacqueline is inspiring entrepreneurs in the developing world to create enterprises that enrich the people around them. She's helping create organizations that deliver clean water, ambulances, and reading glasses . . . and doing it in a scalable way that challenges expectations.

Jacqueline doesn't just love her job leading the Acumen Fund; she's also changing the very face of philanthropy. Her tribe of donors, employees, entrepreneurs, and supporters counts on her leadership to inspire and motivate them.

Geography used to be important. A tribe might be everyone in a certain village, or it might be model-car enthusiasts in Sacramento, or it might be the Democrats in Springfield. Corporations and other organizations have always created their own tribes around their offices or their markets—tribes of employees or customers or parishioners.

Now, the Internet eliminates geography.

This means that existing tribes are bigger, but more important, it means that there are now more tribes, smaller tribes, influential tribes, horizontal and vertical tribes, and tribes that could never have existed before. Tribes you work with, tribes you travel with, tribes you buy with. Tribes that vote, that discuss, that fight. Tribes where everyone knows your name. The professionals at the CIA are a tribe and so are the volunteers at the ACLU.

There's an explosion of new tools available to help lead the tribes we're forming. Facebook and Ning and Meetup and Twitter. Squidoo and Basecamp and Craigslist and e-mail.

There are literally thousands of ways to coordinate and connect groups of people that just didn't exist a generation ago.

All of it is worthless if you don't decide to lead. All of it goes to waste if your leadership is compromised, if you settle, if you don't commit.

Many tribes. Many tools. I'm writing to you about both. The market needs you (*we* need you) and the tools are there, just waiting. All that's missing is you, and your vision and your passion.

In Search of a Movement

Some tribes are stuck. They embrace the status quo and drown out any tribe member who dares to question authority and the accepted order. Big charities, tiny clubs, struggling corporations—they're tribes and they're stuck. I'm not so interested in those tribes. They create little of value and they're sort of boring. Every one of those tribes, though, is a movement waiting to happen, a group of people just waiting to be energized and transformed.

A movement is thrilling. It's the work of many people, all connected, all seeking something better. The new highly leveraged tools of the Net make it easier than ever to create a movement, to make things happen, to get things done.

All that's missing is leadership.

Tribes Aren't So Squishy Anymore

Before the Internet, coordinating and leading a tribe was difficult. It was difficult to get the word out, difficult to coordinate action, difficult to grow quickly. Today, of course, instant communication makes things taut, not squishy. In today's world, Barack Obama can raise $50 million in twenty-eight days. In the nonsquishy tribal world of this decade, Twitter and blogs and online videos and countless other techniques contribute to an entirely new dimension of what it means to be part of a tribe. The new technologies are all designed to connect tribes and to amplify their work.

Please note! Throughout this book, I'm pretty quick to use examples based on the Internet and some of the astonishing new tools that are showing up to enable tribes to be more effective. But the Internet is just a tool, an easy way to enable some tactics. The real power of tribes has nothing to do with the Internet and everything to do with people. You don't need a keyboard to lead . . . you only need the desire to make something happen.

And if you don't have that desire, don't panic. Sometimes it's okay not to take the lead, sometimes it's okay to let someone else speak up and show you the way. The power of this new era is simple: if you want to (need to, must!) lead, then you can. It's easier than ever and we need you. But if this isn't the right moment, if this isn't the right cause, then hold off.

Generous and authentic leadership will always defeat the selfish efforts of someone doing it just because she can.

How Was That Syrah?

Gary Vaynerchuk runs Wine Library TV (http://tv.wine library.com/), and he has a tribe. Millions of people around the world turn to him to narrate their passion for wine. He helps them discover new wines and better understand the wines they love. But Gary doesn't market to this audience, and he doesn't manage them either. He leads a tribe instead. It's an act of generosity and the fuel for a movement, not a marketing stunt. He doesn't push; he leads.

Were people writing about or talking about wine before? Of course. Information has never been difficult to come by. What makes Gary so successful is the way he uses a new medium and new techniques to communicate his passion, to connect people, and to create change. And so a movement grows.

The Tribe Inside

Mich Mathews is the senior vice president of Microsoft's Central Marketing Group. Bill Gates and Steve Ballmer have relied on her to market Microsoft for about a decade.

You've never heard of Mich. She's not a pundit or a

touring personality. Instead, she leads a tribe of thousands of people inside Microsoft who create and shape the company's marketing. The tribe listens to Mich; they respect her and they follow her. The attention paid by this internal tribe is a hard-earned privilege and a valuable responsibility.

This is a book for anyone who chooses to lead a tribe. Inside or out, the possibilities are huge.

The Opportunity

It's simple: there are tribes everywhere now, inside and outside of organizations, in public and in private, in nonprofits, in classrooms, across the planet. Every one of these tribes is yearning for leadership and connection. This is an opportunity for you—an opportunity to find or assemble a tribe and lead it. The question isn't, Is it possible for me to do that? Now, the question is, Will I choose to do it?

For a long time, I've been writing about the fact that everyone is now a marketer. The explosion in media channels, combined with the increased leverage of individuals within organizations, means that just about anyone can influence the marketing of just about everything.

This book says something new. Everyone is not just a marketer—*everyone is now also a leader*. The explosion in tribes, groups, covens, and circles of interest means that anyone who wants to make a difference can.

Without leaders, there are no followers.
You're a leader.
We need you.

Something to Believe In

Tribes are about faith—about belief in an idea and in a community. And they are grounded in respect and admiration for the leader of the tribe and for the other members as well.

Do you believe in what you do? Every day? It turns out that belief happens to be a brilliant strategy.

Three things have happened, pretty much at the same time. All three point to the same (temporarily uncomfortable, but ultimately marvelous) outcome:

1. Many people are starting to realize that they work a lot and that working on stuff they believe in (and making things happen) is much more satisfying than just getting a paycheck and waiting to get fired (or die).

2. Many organizations have discovered that the factory-centric model of producing goods and services is not nearly as profitable as it used to be.

3. Many consumers have decided to spend their money buying things that aren't factory-produced commodities.

And they've decided not to spend their time embracing off-the-shelf ideas. Consumers have decided, instead, to spend time and money on fashion, on stories, on things that matter, and on things they believe in.

So here we are. We live in a world where we have the leverage to make things happen, the desire to do work we believe in, and a marketplace that is begging us to be remarkable. And yet, in the middle of these changes, we still get stuck.

Stuck following archaic rules.

Stuck in industries that not only avoid change but actively fight it.

Stuck in fear of what our boss will say, stuck because we're afraid we'll get into trouble.

Most of all, we're stuck acting like managers or employees, instead of like the leaders we could become. **We're embracing a factory instead of a tribe.**

The irony is that all of this fear used to be useful. Fear of change is built into most organisms, because change is the first sign of risk. Fear of change in a huge factory is appropriate when efficiency is the order of the day. Today, though, the fear that used to protect us at work is now our enemy; it's now the thing standing in the way. Imagine having worked at AOL or a mortgage broker or Sears. It might have been fun for a while, but it's no fun at all when the factory fades.

"How was your day?" is a question that matters a lot more than it seems. It turns out that the people who like their jobs the most are also the ones who are doing the best work, making the greatest impact, and changing the most. Changing the way they see the world, sure, but also changing the world. By challenging the status quo, a cadre of heretics is discovering that one person, just one, can make a huge difference.

Jonathan Ive is having a ball working at Apple, but he's also making a difference. He's leading their design team and feeding the Macintosh tribe with ideas they embrace.

Micah Sifry doesn't just enjoy the work he does every day at the Personal Democracy Forum; he's leading a fundamental change in the way we think about politics. Thousands of people depend on Micah's leadership, and in return, he spends his day engaged in work that matters.

Heretics are the new leaders. The ones who challenge the status quo, who get out in front of their tribes, who create movements.

The marketplace now rewards (and embraces) the heretics. It's clearly more fun to make the rules than to follow them, and for the first time, it's also profitable, powerful, and productive to do just that.

This shift might be bigger than you think. Suddenly, heretics, troublemakers, and change agents aren't merely thorns in our side—they are the keys to our success. Tribes give you leverage. And each of us has more leverage than ever before. I want you to think about the ramifications of the new leverage. I'm hoping you'll see that the most profitable path is also the most reliable, the easiest, and the most fun. Maybe, just maybe, I'll be able to give you a push on the path to becoming a heretic yourself.

Why Should You Lead? And Why Now?

This book weaves together a few big ideas, which, taken together, form an irresistible argument.

With tribes flourishing everywhere, there's a vast shortage of leaders. We need you.

My thesis:

- For the first time ever, everyone in an organization—not just the boss—is expected to lead.
- The very structure of today's workplace means that it's easier than ever to change things and that individuals have more leverage than ever before.
- The marketplace is rewarding organizations and individuals who change things and create remarkable products and services.
- It's engaging, thrilling, profitable, and fun.

- Most of all, there is a tribe of fellow employees or customers or investors or believers or hobbyists or readers just waiting for you to connect them to one another and lead them where they want to go.

Leadership isn't difficult, but you've been trained for years to avoid it. I want to help you realize that you already have all the skills you need to make a huge difference, and I want to sell you on doing it. The best thing is that you don't need to wait until you've got exactly the right job or built the right organization or moved up three rungs on the corporate ladder. You can start right now.

Leadership Is Not Management

In a classic *I Love Lucy* episode, Lucy and Ethel are working on a candy assembly line. As the candies come faster and faster, the two of them panic, stuffing truffles into their mouths to keep up with the onslaught.

They had a management problem.

Management is about manipulating resources to get a known job done. Burger King franchises hire managers. They know exactly what they need to deliver and they are given resources to do it at low cost. Managers manage a process they've seen before, and they react to the outside world, striving to make that process as fast and as cheap as possible.

Leadership, on the other hand, is about creating change that you believe in.

My thesaurus says the best synonym for *leadership* is *management*. Maybe that word used to fit, but no longer. Movements have leaders and movements make things happen.

Leaders have followers. Managers have employees.

Managers make widgets. Leaders make change.

Change? Change is frightening, and to many people who would be leaders, it seems more of a threat than a promise. That's too bad, because the future belongs to our leaders, regardless of where they work or what they do.

It's Good to Be King

In fact, in a stable world, it's *great* to be king. Lots of perks. Not a lot of hassles.

Kings have always worked to maintain stability because that's the best way to stay king. They've traditionally surrounded themselves with a well-fed and well-paid court of supplicants, each of whom has a vested interest in keeping things as they are.

The monarchy has had a huge impact on the way we see the world. Kings taught us about power and about influence and about getting things done. A king assembles his own geographically based tribe and uses power to enforce compliance.

From royalty we learned how to build corporations. And from royalty we learned how to build nonprofits and other organizations as well. Long live the king.

Corporations are traditionally built around the CEO, with all his perks and power. The closer you get to being king/ CEO, the more influence and power you have. The goal of the corporation is to enrich the king and to keep him in power.

And then, recently, something happened.

Marketing changed everything. Marketing created leverage. Marketing certainly changed the status quo. Most of all, marketing freed and energized the tribe.

If the tribe doesn't like the king, they're now free to leave.

The changing status quo isn't such good news for the CEO, just as the changing face of warfare and politics wasn't good news for the crowned heads of Europe a century ago.

Marketing is the act of telling stories about the things we make—stories that sell and stories that spread. Marketing elects presidents, and marketing raises money for charity. Marketing also determines if the CEO stays or goes (Carly Fiorina learned this the hard way). Most of all, marketing influences markets.

Marketing used to be about advertising, and advertising

is expensive. Today, marketing is about engaging with the tribe and delivering products and services with stories that spread.

Today, the market doesn't want the same thing it wanted yesterday. Marketing, a hundred years of incessant marketing, has drilled into us a thirst for what's new. And new isn't so stable, is it?

Stability Is an Illusion

Marketing changed the idea of stability. It's human nature—we still assume the world is stable, still assume that Google will be number one in five years, that we'll type on keyboards and fly on airplanes, that China will keep growing, and that the polar ice cap won't really be melted in six years.

And we're wrong.

We're wrong because the dynamics of marketing and storytelling and the incessant drumbeat of advertising have taught us to be restless in the face of stability. And the Internet just amplifies this lesson.

No one watches a mediocre YouTube video they've seen before. No one passes on a boring e-mail. No one invests in a stock that's boring, with few prospects for big growth.

Here's what's changed: some people admire the new and the stylish far more than they respect the proven state of affairs. And more often than not, these fad-focused early adopters are the people who buy and the people who talk. As a result, new ways of doing things, new jobs, new opportunities, and new faces become ever more important.

Marketing, the verb, changed the market. The market is now a lot less impressed with average stuff for average people, and the market is a lot less impressed with loud and flashy and expensive advertising. Today, the market wants change.

"Established 1906" used to be important. Now, apparently, it's a liability.

The rush from stability is a huge opportunity for you.

Partisans

It's a criticism when you throw that word at a politician, but all tribes are made up of partisans, the more partisan the better. If you're a middle-of-the-roader, you don't bother joining a tribe.

Partisans want to make a difference. Partisans want something to happen (and something else *not* to happen). Leaders lead when they take positions, when they connect with their tribes, and when they help the tribe connect to itself.

Making a Ruckus

The old rule was simple: The best way to grow an organization was to be reliable and consistent and trusted, and bit by bit, gain market share. The enemy was rapid change, because that led to uncertainty and to risk and to failure. People turned and ran.

Take a look at the top fifty charities on the *Chronicle of Philanthropy*'s top four hundred charity list. During the last forty years, only a handful of charities on this list have changed. Why? Because donors didn't want to take risks.

The business world has a long history of conservative tribes, of groups of people who relish the status quo. The big news is that this has changed. People yearn for change, they relish being part of a movement, and they talk about things that are remarkable, not boring.

Take a look at the Yugo and the Renault and the Sterling—manufactured by companies that decades ago tried to bring new ideas to the U.S. car market and failed. Why? Because drivers then didn't want to buy a car that might disappear. It was no fun to work at these companies because they were fighting an uphill battle. Better to go work for General Motors.

New rule: If you want to grow, you need to find customers who are willing to join you or believe in you or donate to you or support you. And guess what? The only customers willing to do that are looking for something new. The growth comes from change and light and noise.

The Tesla Roadster is a $100,000 electric supercar, built in Silicon Valley. Impossible to consider thirty years ago.

Now, it's sold out. The company has assembled a tribe—eager customers, cheerleaders, and vicarious fans.

The Prius Hybrid is a new car based on a hundred-year-old technology that no domestic carmaker cared enough about to develop. Today, there's a long list of brands following Toyota. The tribe has turned into a movement. This is astounding—the biggest, staidest consumer product industry turning itself upside down in just a few years.

If struggling, high-overhead car companies can launch a technology and find market acceptance, imagine what you can do with this new leverage.

What do you do for a living? What do you make?

Leaders make a ruckus.

Leading from the Bottom

The skeptical among us look at the idea of leadership and we hesitate.

We hesitate because it feels like something we need to be ordained to do. That without authority, we can't lead. That big organizations reserve leadership for the CEO, not for us.

Perhaps you work at a big organization. Perhaps you feel as though there's just too much resistance to change. Here's a question: Is your organization stiffer than the Pentagon? More bureaucratic or formalized?

Thomas Barnett changed the Pentagon. From the bottom. No, he wasn't on KP duty, but he was close. He had no status, no rank—he was just a researcher with a big idea.

Here's what the *Wall Street Journal* said:

Mr. Barnett overhauled the concept to address more directly the post-9/11 world. The result is a three-hour PowerPoint presentation that more resembles performance art than a Pentagon briefing. It's making Mr. Barnett, 41 years old, a key figure in the debate currently raging about what the modern military should look like. Senior military officials say his decidedly controversial ideas are influencing the way the Pentagon views its enemies, vulnerabilities and future structure.

It's simple, really. Barnett led a tribe that was passionate about change. He galvanized them, inspired them, and connected them, through his idea.

One man with no authority suddenly becomes a key figure. Tribes give each of us the very same opportunity. Skill and attitude are essential. Authority is not. In fact, authority can get in the way.

The Grateful Dead . . . and Jack

It's worth taking a second to think about what it really means to be a tribe.

In *Permission Marketing*, years ago, I wrote about how marketers must earn the right to deliver anticipated, personal, and relevant messages to people who want to get them. And that's still correct, as far as it goes.

But tribes go much further. That's because in addition to the messages that go from the marketer or the leader to the tribe, there are the messages that go sideways, from member to member, and back to the leader as well.

The Grateful Dead understood this. They created concerts to allow people not just to hear their music, but to hear it *together*. That's where the tribe part comes in.

I just heard about Jack, an "occasional restaurant" run by Danielle Sucher and Dave Turner in Brooklyn. They open the restaurant only about twenty times a year, on Saturday nights. By appointment. Go online and you can see the menu in advance. Then, you book and pay if you want to go.

Instead of seeking diners for their dishes, Danielle and Dave get to create dishes for their diners. Instead of serving anonymous patrons, they throw a party.

Danielle is the food columnist for the popular Gothamist Web site, and she and Dave run the food blog Habeas Brûlée. That means they already interact with the tribe. It means that once the restaurant is up and running, it becomes the central clearinghouse, the place to hang out with the other tribe members.

If the food is daring and the service is generous, Jack can't fail.

The Market Requires Change and That Requires Leadership

If leadership is the ability to create change your tribe believes in, and the market demands change, then the market demands leaders.

Managers manage by using the authority the factory gives them. You listen to your manager or you lose your job. A manager can't make change because that's not his job. His job is to complete tasks assigned to him by someone else in the factory.

Leaders, on the other hand, don't care very much for organizational structure or the official blessing of whatever factory they work for. They use passion and ideas to lead people, as opposed to using threats and bureaucracy to manage them. Leaders must become aware of how the organization works, because this awareness allows them to change it.

Leadership doesn't always start at the top, but it always manages to affect the folks at the top. In fact, most organizations are waiting for someone like you to lead them.

What Does It Take to Create a Movement?

If we look at two Nobel Prize winners and their movements—Muhammad Yunus and Al Gore—some parallels become clear, and they directly relate to the tactics available to you as you lead your tribe.

Microfinance as a tool to fight poverty and the effort to recognize and stem global warming have both become movements. But as Yasmina Zaidman, at the Acumen Fund, told me, both problems (and their solutions!) were recognized more than thirty years ago. We weren't lacking the answer—Muhammad Yunus had it all along. So why did it take thirty years for the idea to gain steam?

The answer, as you've probably guessed, is that there's a difference between telling people what to do and inciting a movement. The movement happens when people talk to one another, when ideas spread within the community, and most of all, when peer support leads people to do what they always knew was the right thing.

Great leaders create movements by empowering the tribe to communicate. They establish the foundation for people to make connections, as opposed to commanding people to follow them.

This is how Skype spread around the world. Cofounder Niklas Zennström understood that overthrowing the tyranny of the phone companies was too big a project for a small company. But if he could empower the tribe to do it themselves, to connect to one another and to spread the word, he would be able to incite a movement.

Malcolm Gladwell wrote about the fall of the Berlin Wall, and it involved much the same dynamic. The collapse of East Germany wasn't the work of one hardworking activist. Instead, it was the gradual but inexorable growth of the tribe, a loosely coordinated movement of activists that gained in force until it couldn't be stopped.

One after another, intractable problems fall in the face of movements.

Improving a Tribe

As we saw earlier, it takes only two things to turn a group of people into a tribe:

- A shared interest
- A way to communicate

The communication can be one of four kinds:

- Leader to tribe
- Tribe to leader
- Tribe member to tribe member
- Tribe member to outsider

So a leader can help increase the effectiveness of the tribe and its members by

- transforming the shared interest into a passionate goal and desire for change;
- providing tools to allow members to tighten their communications; and
- leveraging the tribe to allow it to grow and gain new members.

Most leaders focus only on the third tactic. A bigger tribe somehow equals a better tribe. In fact, the first two tactics almost always lead to more impact. Every action you take as a leader can affect these three elements, and the challenge is to figure out which one to maximize.

The American Automobile Association has millions of members, but it arguably has far less impact on the world than do the two thousand people who go to the TED conference each year. One is about big and the other is about change.

The National Rifle Association has a huge impact on the political culture of the United States, far in excess of the organization's actual size. That's because the tribe is extraordinarily well connected, communicating up, down, *and* sideways, and because they have a passionate mission, not just a common idea.

The new tools and technologies available to groups are

transforming what it means to think of tribal communication. Smart leaders are grabbing those tools and putting them to work.

What Tribes Leave Behind

Build a company and you'll leave a trace. A factory, advertising, the nonrecyclable junk produced as a result of your efforts.

Thinking about stuff is easy because we can see and touch and hold stuff. Stuff seems to matter, because it's here, right now.

Tribes, though, aren't about stuff. They're about connection.

One of my favorite organizations, the Acumen Fund, just celebrated its seventh anniversary. This nonprofit funds entrepreneurs in the developing world, using trade and ownership and commerce as a replacement for achievement-stifling aid.

Acumen makes connections. It is growing a tribe of committed, talented people who are spreading a message of empowerment, respect, and growth. Here's what amazed me, though: unlike the residue of stuff, the tribal connections you can create with leadership grow; they don't fade. As the organization matures and touches more people, those connections lead to more connections. The tribe thrives; it delivers value and it spreads. Internet folks call this viral activity, or a virtuous cycle. The better you do, the better you do. Connections lead to connections. Great ideas spread.

Anatomy of a Movement

Senator Bill Bradley defines a movement as having three elements:

1. A narrative that tells a story about who we are and the future we're trying to build

2. A connection between and among the leader and the tribe

3. Something to do—the fewer limits, the better

Too often organizations fail to do anything but the third.

Wikipedia

How did Wikipedia become one of the top ten sites on the Internet? It has only about a dozen full-time employees and had no source of revenue other than small donations.

The way that Jimmy Wales, Wikipedia's cofounder, built the tribe is instructive. He attracted a small group of people (only five thousand people account for the vast majority of work on the articles on the site) and engaged them in a vision. He didn't tell them what to do. He didn't manage the effort; he led it.

Wales connected the tribe members to one another with ever-evolving technology that made it easier and easier for them to engage and communicate. And he gave the tribe a platform they could use to engage the outside world.

That's it—three steps: motivate, connect, and leverage.

Leading from the Bottom (with a Newsletter)

In 1984, at the age of twenty-four, I joined a tiny software company called Spinnaker. Based in Cambridge, Massachusetts, we were crazy enough to embrace the audacious goal of inventing the first generation of educational computer games. I was the thirtieth employee.

After my summer internship, Spinnaker offered me a job starting a new brand. They wanted me to acquire science fiction stories and turn them into literary adventure games. Byron Preiss had already sold us the rights to *Fahrenheit 451* and a few other novels, and I had to acquire others and turn them all into products ready for stores nationwide. The problem was that no one worked for me. No secretary, no staff, no programmers.

Spinnaker was busy building dozens of products, and about

forty programmers in the Engineering Department were allocated on a rotating basis to various projects. I was lent precisely three programmers. I needed more, a lot more, if I was going to make my Christmas ship date.

So I started a newsletter. The newsletter highlighted the work of every person who worked on one of my products. It highlighted their breakthroughs and talked about the new ground we were breaking (music! in a game!). I made photocopies and distributed the newsletter to the interoffice mailbox of every person in the company—by then about a hundred people.

Twice a week, the newsletter went out. Twice a week, I talked about our quest. Twice a week, I chronicled the amazing work of our tiny tribe. The newsletter connected the tribe members. It turned a disparate group of career engineers into a working community.

Within a month, six engineers had defected to the tribe, working with me in their spare time. Then it was twenty. Soon, every person in the entire department was either assigned to my project or moonlighting on it. We shipped five products in time for Christmas, and every one went Gold, selling millions of dollars' worth of copies and saving the company.

Did engineers switch because of the newsletter? Of course not. They switched for the journey. They wanted to be part of something that mattered. Twenty years later, people on that team still talk about what we built. And I, the twenty-four-year-old with no experience and no staff, got to go on the ride of a lifetime.

Is that all I did? Launch a newsletter? Of course not. I did difficult things, pushed obstacles out of the way, lived and breathed the project, and injected it with a soul. Thirty of us slept in the office every night for a month to make the ship date. Twenty-nine highly skilled technical people and me. Everyone had a job to do that month and mine was to help everyone else communicate.

Everything I did was for *us*, not for *me*. I didn't manage; I led.

Crowds and Tribes

Two different things:

A crowd is a tribe without a leader.

A crowd is a tribe without communication.

Most organizations spend their time marketing to the crowd. Smart organizations assemble the tribe.

Crowds are interesting, and they can create all sorts of worthwhile artifacts and market effects. But tribes are longer lasting and more effective.

Marketing Changes Everything, but It Mostly Changes the Market

The market wants you to be remarkable. The most important tribes are bored with yesterday and demand tomorrow. Most of all, the market has demonstrated that ideas that spread win, and the ideas that are spreading are the remarkable ones.

For fifty years, established brands with efficient factories and effective marketing carried the day. Pepsi, the Salvation Army, and the local hardware store were the cornerstones of the marketplace. Suddenly, though, the oldest brands are no longer the fastest-growing ones. Suddenly, the most experienced businesspeople are no longer the most successful ones. And suddenly, the safest jobs are not so safe anymore.

The marketplace has raised its voice. It's now clear that we want novelty and style and, most of all, stuff that's great. If you want us to follow you, don't be boring.

"Good enough" stopped being good enough a long time ago. So why not be great?

The Difference Between Average and Mediocre

Management often works to maintain the status quo, to deliver average products to average people. In a stable environment, this is exactly the right strategy. Build reliability and predictability, cut costs, and make a profit.

Traditional marketing, the marketing of push, understands this. The most stable thing to do is push a standard product to a standard audience and succeed with discounts or distribution.

But for tribes, average can mean mediocre. Not worth seeking out. Boring.

Life's too short to fight the forces of change. Life's too short to hate what you do all day. Life's way too short to make mediocre stuff. And almost everything that's standard is now viewed as mediocre.

Is there a difference between average and mediocre? Not so much. Average stuff is taken for granted, not talked about, and certainly not sought out.

The end result of this is that many people (many really good people) spend all day trying to defend what they do, trying to sell what they've always sold, and trying to prevent their organizations from being devoured by the forces of the new. It must be wearing them out. Defending mediocrity is exhausting.

How Many Fans Do You Have?

In an article posted on his Technium Web site, Kevin Kelly brilliantly described the world of "1,000 True Fans." A true fan, he argues, is a member of the tribe who cares deeply about you and your work. That person will cross the street to buy from you or bring a friend to hear you or invest a little extra to support you.

An individual artist needs only a thousand true fans in her tribe. It's enough.

It's enough because a thousand fans will bring you enough attention and support to make a great living, to reach more people, to do great work. It's enough because a thousand fans, true fans, form a tribe.

A true fan brings three friends with him to a John Mayer concert or to the opening of a Chuck Close exhibit. A true fan pays extra to own the first edition, or buys the hardcover, instead of just browsing around on the Web site. Most important, a true fan connects with other true fans and amplifies the noise the artist makes.

A corporation or a nonprofit or a church may need more than that—perhaps a million fans if you're Starbucks, or fifteen million if you're running for president. But it's beyond doubt that there's a number—you can figure out what it is—and it's probably fewer people than you imagine.

Too many organizations care about numbers, not fans. They care about hits or turnstile clicks or media mentions. What they're missing is the depth of commitment and interconnection that true fans deliver. Instead of always being on the hunt for one more set of eyeballs, true leaders have figured out that the real win is in turning a casual fan into a true one.

Fans, true fans, are hard to find and precious. Just a few can change everything. What they demand, though, is generosity and bravery.

Twitter and Trust and Tribes and True Fans

Most people who see Twitter.com don't get it. It seems invasive or time consuming or even dumb.

The converts, though, understand the true power of Twitter. Twitter is deceptively simple: it's a Web protocol that makes it easy to instant-message people with short notes like "going to the gym." In fact, the limit is 140 characters, about half the length of this paragraph.

The difference between an instant message and twits, though, is that your instant message goes to one person and a twit goes to anyone who has chosen to follow you. Example: Laura Fitton, a young mom in Boston, has thousands of people following her on Twitter. Every time she types in a short blurb, they see it.

Over time, twit by twit, Laura has built trust, which has led to a successful career as a consultant and a worldwide speaking practice. She's met fascinating people and changed the way her tribe sees the world. She now has true fans, people who seek her out and talk about her.

Laura couldn't have done this with one speech or one blog

post. But by consistently touching a tribe of people with generosity and insight, she's earned the right to lead.

Personally, I can't imagine the technology mattering much. Blogs and Twitter and all manner of other tools will come and go, possibly by the time you read this. The tactics are irrelevant, and the technology will always be changing. The essential lesson is that every day it gets easier to tighten the relationship you have with the people who choose to follow you.

The Status Quo

Organizations that destroy the status quo win.

Individuals who push their organizations, who inspire other individuals to change the rules, thrive. Again, we're back to leadership, which can come from anyone, anywhere in the organization.

The status quo could be the time that "everyone knows" it takes you to ship an order, or the commission rate that "everyone knows" an agent ought to be paid. The status quo might be the way everyone expects a product to be packaged or the pricing model that everyone accepts because it's been around so long.

Whatever the status quo is, changing it gives you the opportunity to be remarkable.

Initiative = Happiness

Look around. You'll see that the marketplace (every market-place) rewards innovation: things that are fresh, stylish, re-markable, and new.

The fastest-growing churches are the newest ones. The best-selling books are always the surprise hits that come out of nowhere. The tax shelter that everyone is talking about is the one based on the latest rulings.

Products and services like those require initiative to pro-duce. You can't manage your way to initiative.

Interesting side effect: creating products and services that are remarkable is fun. Doing work that's fun is engaging. So not surprisingly, making things that are successful is a great way to spend your time.

There you go: initiative = happiness.

Crowbars

With a long enough crowbar, you can rip nails out of a board.

With a long enough teeter-totter, you can lift a sumo wres-tler off the ground.

With enough leverage, you can change your company, your industry, and the world.

The levers just got longer (for everyone). The Web and

word of mouth and viruses and outsourcing and the long tail and the other factors involved in social media mean that everyone (every person, all six billion of us) has far more power than ever before. The king and the status quo are in big trouble.

Wait. You might have glossed over that last paragraph—perhaps because it's so short but especially because it's so challenging.

What I'm saying is that one person can make a video that reaches fifty million viewers.

What I'm saying is that one person can invent a pricing model that turns an industry upside down.

What I'm saying is that one person—okay, what I really mean is *you*—has everything. Everything you need to build something far bigger than yourself. The people around you realize this, and they are ready to follow if you're ready to lead.

Scott Beale's Party

Here's a simple example of a tribe enabled by new technology. Scott Beale is an impresario with a long history of innovation and leadership. His company, Laughing Squid, does everything from Web hosting to T-shirts, from laser engraving to arts listings. In short, he leads an eclectic tribe.

At the SXSW conference in 2008, Scott got tired of

waiting in line to get into the Google party. So he walked down the street, found a deserted bar, grabbed some tables in the back, and fired up his cell phone. Using Twitter, he announced: "Alta Vista Party at Ginger Man." Within minutes, eight people showed up. Shortly thereafter, fifty. Then there was a line out the door.

No, it's not a political movement. Sure, it's a tribe. The energy and connection of the tribe are palpable. Multiply this effect by a million similar tribes and now you understand what's happening. Tribes are just waiting to be turned into movements. (And occasionally to stop to have a beer together.)

It's important to note that Twitter merely enabled the event; it didn't cause it to occur. Unless Scott had earned the respect and permission of the tribe that follows him, he would have been all alone at the bar. The party didn't take four minutes to organize; it took four years.

A Brief History of the Factory, Part 1 (the Beginning)

Two things conspired to bring us the factory.

The first is pretty obvious: factories are efficient. Starting a factory and filling it with factory workers is a good way to make a profit.

By "factory," I don't necessarily mean a place with heavy machinery, greasy floors, and a din. I mean any organization that cranks out a product or a service, does it with measurable output, and tries to reduce costs as it goes. I mean any job where your boss tells you what to do and how to do it.

The second reason we have factories has nothing to do with efficiency and a lot to do with human nature. Part of us wants stability. We want the absence of responsibility that a factory job can give us. The idea of "I'm doing what you told me to" is very compelling, especially if the alternative is foraging for food or begging on the streets.

So when factories showed up, we ran to join them.

On a recent trip I took to India, this mind-set was made crystal clear. Ask almost anyone there what the perfect job would be, and the answer is: working as a government bureaucrat. Not only do you have air-conditioning, but you aren't even asked to take initiative. The job is steady, the pay is good, and there are no surprises.

The factory is part of the fabric of our lives. It's there because it pays, and it's there because it's steady, and it's there because we want it. What you won't find in a factory is a motivated tribe making a difference. And what you won't find waiting outside the factory is a tribe of customers, excited about what's to come.

A Brief History of the Factory, Part II (the End)

Somewhere along the way, perhaps when twenty thousand Ford workers lost their jobs in one day, or when it became clear that soft drink companies were losing all their growth to upstarts, the factory advantage began to fade.

It wasn't so safe to have a factory job after all.

And in an age of leverage, in an age where smarts and style were beating machines every time, doing what your boss said wasn't so enticing either.

If you could have any job in the world, what would it be?

Did you say, "A low-level bureaucrat working in the Social Security office in Yonkers, New York"?

Did you say, "A midlevel supervisor at a struggling GM plant in Ohio"?

Did you say, "Fry cook at McDonald's"?

Somehow, I doubt it.

Now, it seems, the air-conditioning and the illusion of deniability aren't worth so much. Now, when we envision our dream jobs, we're imagining someone who reaps huge rewards as a result of her insight. Or someone who has control over what he does all day, creating products or services that he's actually proud of. It certainly involves having authority over your time and your effort and having input into what you do.

None of which have anything to do with working in a factory.

So Is It Really a "Free Agent Nation"?

The author Dan Pink coined the term Free Agent Nation to describe a movement of smart people leaving organizations to go out on their own.

That's not what I'm talking about, though.

Organizations are more important than ever before. It's the factories we don't need.

Organizations give us the ability to create complex products. They provide the muscle and consistency necessary to get things to market and to back them up. Most important, organizations have the scale to care for large tribes.

But organizations don't have to be factories, not anymore. Factories are easy to outsource. Factories can slow you down. The organizations of the future are filled with smart, fast, flexible people on a mission. The thing is, that requires leadership.

If you don't have a time-tested manual, you can't manage your way through this. In unstable times, growth comes from leaders who create change and engage their organizations, instead of from managers who push their employees to do more for less.

The F Word

So if tribes reward innovation . . .

   . . . and if initiators are happier . . .

   . . . then why doesn't everyone do it?

Because of fear.

I've encountered thousands (it might be tens of thousands) of people walking around with great ideas. Some of the ideas really are great; some are merely pretty good. There doesn't seem to be a shortage of ideas. Ordinary folks can dream up remarkable stuff fairly easily.

What's missing is the will to make the ideas happen.

In a battle between two ideas, the best one doesn't necessarily win. No, the idea that wins is the one with the most fearless heretic behind it.

A lot of us would like to believe that there's a Bureau of Idea Approval, or the BIA if you like acronyms. The BIA sits in judgment of ideas and blesses the best ones. Go ahead and hone your remarkable concept, submit it to the BIA, and let them do the rest.

Alas, it's not going to happen like that any time soon.

Thinking Your Way Out of the Fear

Fear's an emotion, no doubt about it. One of the strongest, oldest, and most hardwired.

The media love to glamorize the rare downfall of the heretic who doesn't quite make it. We're already primed to hear about the person who got into trouble, who lost his job, his house, his family—his happiness—because he had the hubris and audacity to challenge the status quo. And since we're eager for this news, we notice it the few times it happens.

What's interesting about the folks I meet who are engaged and are clearly heretics is that they've actively talked themselves out of the fear. I mean, the fear is still there, but it's drowned out by a different story.

It's the story of success, of drive, of doing something that matters. It's an intellectual story about what the world (or your industry or your project) needs and how your insight can help make a difference.

I believe you can talk over the fear, laying out a game plan that makes the fear obsolete. It's not about some clever tactic or a better way to write a memo to your boss. It's about making it clear to yourself (and to others) that the world is now demanding that we change. And fast.

Wait.

We need to stop again. It's clear that just a few paragraphs aren't going to be sufficient to undo a lifetime of having fear beaten into you.

So stop for a second and think about this. The only shortcut in this book, the only technique or how-to or inside info is this: the levers are here. The proof is here. The power is here. The only thing holding you back is your own fear.

Not easy to admit, but essential to understand.

The Peter Principle Revisited

Dr. Laurence Peter is famous for proposing that "in a hierarchy every employee tends to rise to his level of incompetence." In other words, when you do a great job, you get promoted. And that process repeats itself until finally you end up in a job you can't handle.

I'd like to paraphrase the Peter Principle. I think what actually happens is that "in every organization everyone rises to the level at which they become paralyzed with fear."

The essence of leadership is being aware of your fear (and seeing it in the people you wish to lead). No, it won't go away, but awareness is the key to making progress.

When It All Falls Apart

It's so common, but it doesn't really have a name. I'm talking about the people who struggle for years but never seem to get anywhere. This lack of traction is often most noticeable in small businesses, but you'll also find it at well-meaning nonprofits and large corporations.

You work and work, following all the rules, pushing really hard but nothing happens. All pain, no gain.

What's happening?

I think these people are becoming ever better at following, but are never learning to lead. They're following instructions, following directions, following the pack, and honing their skills—but hiding. Hiding from the fear of leading.

When you are leading a tribe, a tribe that you belong to, the benefits increase, the work gets easier, and the results are more obvious. That's the best reason to overcome the fear.

Worth Criticizing

A remarkable product or service is like a purple cow. Brown cows are boring; purple ones are worth mentioning. Those ideas spread; those organizations grow. The essence of what's happening in the market today revolves around creating purple cows.

Here's the marketing math:

Ideas that spread, win.

Boring ideas don't spread. Boring organizations don't grow.

Working in an environment that's static is no fun.

Even worse, working for an organization that is busy fighting off change is horrible.

So why haven't you and your team launched as many purple cows as you'd like?

Fear of Failure Is Overrated

Fear of failure is actually overrated as an excuse. Why? Because if you work for someone, then, more often than not, the actual cost of the failure is absorbed by the organization, not by you. If your product launch fails, they're not going to fire you. The company will make a bit less money and will move on.

What people are afraid of isn't failure. It's blame. Criticism.

We choose not to be remarkable because we're worried about criticism. We hesitate to create innovative movies, launch new human resource initiatives, design a menu that makes diners take notice, or give an audacious sermon because we're worried, deep down, that someone will hate it and call us on it.

"That's the stupidest thing I've ever heard!" "What a waste of money." "Who's responsible for this?"

Sometimes the criticism doesn't even have to be that obvious. The fear of hearing "I'm surprised you launched this without doing more research" is enough to get many people to do a lot more research, to study something to death, and then kill it. Hey, at least you didn't get criticized.

Fear of criticism is a powerful deterrent because the criticism doesn't actually have to occur for the fear to set in. Watch a few people get criticized for being innovative, and it's pretty easy to convince yourself that the very same thing will happen to you if you're not careful.

Constructive criticism, of course, is a terrific tool. If a critic tells you, "I don't like it" or "This is disappointing," he's done no good at all. In fact, quite the opposite is true. He's used his power to injure without giving you any information to help you do better next time. Worse, he hasn't given those listening any data with which to make a thoughtful decision on their own. Not only that, but by refusing to reveal the basis for his criticism, he's being a coward, because there's no way to challenge his opinion.

I admit it. When I get a bad review, my feelings are hurt. After all, it would be nice if every critic said a title of mine was a breakthrough, an inspirational, thoughtful book that explains how everything works.

But sometimes they don't. Which is about enough to ruin my day.

But it's *not* enough. It's not enough to ruin my day because I realize that my book got noticed. Most people loved it. A few hated it. But by and large, most books are ignored.

One bad review doesn't ruin my day because I realize what a badge of honor it is to get a bit of criticism at all. It means that I confounded expectations—that I didn't deliver the sequel or the simple, practical guide that some expected. It means that, in fact, I did something worth remarking on.

The lesson here is this: if I had written a boring book, there'd be no criticism. No conversation. The products and services that get talked about are the ones that are worth talking about.

How was your day? If your answer is "fine," then I don't think you were leading.

So the challenge, as you contemplate your next opportunity to be boring or remarkable, is to answer these two questions:

1. "If I get criticized for this, will I suffer any measurable impact? Will I lose my job, get hit upside the head with a softball bat, or lose important friendships?" If the only side effect of the criticism is that you will feel bad about the criticism, then you have to compare that bad feeling with the benefits you'll get from actually doing something worth doing. Being remarkable is exciting, fun, profitable, and great for your career. Feeling bad wears off.

   And then, once you've compared the bad feeling and the benefits, and you've sold yourself on taking the remarkable path, answer this one:

2. How can I create something that critics will criticize?

The Cult of the Heretic

Heretics are engaged, passionate, and more powerful and happier than everyone else. And they have a tribe that they support (and that supports them in turn).

Challenging the status quo requires a commitment, both public and private. It involves reaching out to others and putting your ideas on the line. (Or pinning your Ninety-five Theses to the church door.)

Heretics *must* believe. More than anyone else in an organization, it's the person who's challenging the status quo, the one who is daring to be great, who is truly present and not just punching a clock who must have confidence in her beliefs.

Can you imagine Steve Jobs showing up for the paycheck? It's nice to get paid. It's essential to believe.

Should They Build a Statue of You?

How much ego is involved in being a leader?

David Chang is a fantastic chef with a loyal tribe. His restaurants are blogged about incessantly and people spend hours trying to get in to them. They take photos of the items he makes and post them online, together with reviews like "David Chang is a genius."

It's clear to me that if they built statues for chefs, they'd build one for David.

But is David doing it for the glory, or is he doing it for the tribe? I think you know the answer—great leaders focus on the tribe and only the tribe.

Pema Chodron is a Buddhist nun working in a monastery in Nova Scotia. Millions of people across the world revere her work, read her books, listen to her recordings, and visit her if they can. Is she a raging egomaniac? Of course not. Listen to her for three minutes and you'll know that she's not doing what she does for glory; she's doing it to help.

Which is true of all great leaders, from David Chang in his New York City kitchen to Nancy Pearl, Seattle's favorite librarian. They're generous. They exist to help the tribe find something, to enable the tribe to thrive. But they understand that the most powerful way to enable is to be statueworthy: by getting out front, by making a point, by challenging convention, and by speaking up. Those are brave acts, and bravery begets statues.

It's easy to hesitate when confronted with the feeling that maybe you're getting too much attention. Great leaders are able to reflect the light onto their teams, their tribes. Great leaders don't want the attention, but they use it. They use it to unite the tribe and to reinforce its sense of purpose.

When you abuse the attention, you are taking something from the tribe. When Fidel Castro gave six- or seven-hour-long speeches (with mandatory attendance), he was diminishing the energy of his tribe. When a CEO takes the spoils of royalty and starts acting like a selfish monarch, he's no longer leading. He's taking.

The World's Best Coach

Watching Meghan McDonald coach the members of Team Rock is hardly awe-inspiring. Mostly, she just talks quietly, one on one, to someone who needs to hear from her. Over the course of a few hours, Meghan will have dozens of conversations like that. She occasionally talks to the entire team, but she never raises her voice. No one cries, no one is belittled, no one is bullied.

After just a few weeks, amazing things start to happen. The members of the team start coaching each other. A ten-year-old novice offers a pointer to a veteran recently back from the national competition. Meghan leaves the building, and practice continues.

Sports analogies rarely work for me. They're too unrealistic, too testosterone filled for the real world. Meghan, however, isn't just a coach. She's someone who understands authentic leadership, and she realizes what it means to create a tribe.

She doesn't lead the way other people lead. And that's fine, because there isn't a right technique, a proven tactic, a right way and a wrong way. Deciding to lead, not manage, is the critical choice.

Meghan connects and inspires. She doesn't manage.

Tighter

The first thing a leader can focus on is the act of tightening the tribe.

It's tempting to make the tribe bigger, to get more members, to spread the word. This pales, however, when juxtaposed with the effects of a tighter tribe. A tribe that communicates more quickly, with alacrity and emotion, is a tribe that thrives.

A tighter tribe is one that is more likely to hear its leader, and more likely still to coordinate action and ideas across the members of the tribe.

Steve Jobs at Apple has tightened the tribe of Apple fanatics in a variety of ways. By creating substantial new products and announcing them online, he's made it a ritual for Apple fanatics to "tune in" to hear what's new. Within hours of a new product announcement, the word has spread to millions or even tens of millions of users—all electronically, all online. At the same time, Apple has enjoyed an interesting side effect of Jobs's obsession with secrecy about new products: online rumor sites and speculation further fuel the conversations among Apple fans. Users will prototype imagined products and share pictures and even dig up obscure patents to prove their points.

This tightening can happen without technology, and it can happen when there is no profit motive. Keith Ferrazzi leads a tribe of smart celebrities and opinion leaders—from Meg Ryan to Ben Zander—and he leads this unleadable group merely by tightening the tribe. He introduces people. He invites them to dinner. He finds areas of common interest and then gets out of the way.

Tactics and Tools for Tightness

The Internet and the explosion in social media have made it easier than ever to market.

The first kind of marketing, the act of spreading the word and reaching the unreached, allows tribes of all sorts to form. Sites like Meetup.com and Craigslist make it easy for people who aren't connected to become connected.

I'm more interested in the second kind of marketing, the act of tightening your organization and spreading the word within the tribe. A blog is an easy way to see this method in action. A blogger has a free, nearly effortless tool to send regular (daily? hourly?) messages to the people who want to read them. And with comments and trackbacks, the members of the tribe can talk back—and to each other. Discussions take place, ideas are shared, decisions are made—quickly.

I could write an entire book about the power of a blog to disseminate a leader's ideas. An unpublished poet, previously doomed to railing against the system, is now published (if he wants to be). If the ideas are great, they'll spread. The spread of these ideas can attract a tribe, and the poet goes from anonymity to leadership.

Blogs can work within existing organizations as well. I needed a photocopied newsletter to galvanize the engineers I worked with in 1984; you can use a blog and reach more people, more powerfully and for free.

Internet companies have taken the original idea behind blogs and amplified it into a set of tools that anyone can use to tighten a tribe.

With Twitter, tiny driplike updates reach the thousands of people who are waiting to hear from you and follow your lead.

Facebook goes in the opposite direction of Twitter. Instead of forcing you to use just a few characters, it enables a huge range of images, text, and connections to be created. Facebook surfaces what some are calling the social graph. Who you know, how you know them, who knows whom. It takes the hidden world of tribes and illuminates it with bright digital light.

Basecamp is a third form of online interaction, very different from Twitter and Facebook in that it's quite deliberate, perfect for managing projects and tracking work. By accessing the stuff that used to be in private e-mails or hand-written journals, Basecamp makes it easy for the entire tribe to track progress and feel the momentum that you're building.

Nothing online is even close to a substitute for the hard work and generosity that comes from leadership. But these tools make leadership more powerful and productive, regardless of who's in your tribe.

Discomfort

Leadership is scarce because few people are willing to go through the discomfort required to lead. This scarcity makes leadership valuable. If everyone tries to lead all the time, not much happens. It's discomfort that creates the leverage that makes leadership worthwhile.

In other words, if everyone could do it, they would, and it wouldn't be worth much.

It's uncomfortable to stand up in front of strangers.

It's uncomfortable to propose an idea that might fail.

It's uncomfortable to challenge the status quo.

It's uncomfortable to resist the urge to settle.

When you identify the discomfort, you've found the place where a leader is needed.

If you're not uncomfortable in your work as a leader, it's almost certain you're not reaching your potential as a leader.

Followers

Of course, a tribe needs followers too. An organization, any organization, needs people who aren't just willing to follow, but are *eager* to follow.

I think, though, it's a mistake to believe that your best tribe recruits are blind sheep. Folks who do nothing but mindlessly follow instructions let you down in two ways.

First, they're not going to do the local leadership required when tribe members interact. They're going to be so busy following the playbook that they'll hesitate about engaging in the interactions that make a tight tribe such a vibrant organization. People don't engage merely to remind one another of the status quo. Instead, they eagerly engage when they want something to improve. This microleadership is essential to the health of your organization.

Second, they're not going to do a very good job of recruiting new members to your tribe. That's because evangelism requires leadership. Leading someone toward giving up one worldview and embracing yours isn't easy and it's not always comfortable. Consider any vibrant group—political activists, nonprofit volunteers, or brand fanatics. In each case, it's the microleaders in the trenches and their enthusiastic followers who make the difference, not the honcho who is ostensibly running the group.

Leaning In, Backing Off, Doing Nothing

Groups create vacuums—small pockets where stasis sets in, where nothing is happening. Imagine a cocktail party in its early stages, where everyone is standing around, waiting for something to happen. Or a marketplace before it opens, filled with shoppers but with all the stores boarded up, with nothing to create energy or excitement. There are no tribes here, only isolated individuals in groups with no motion.

Leaders figure out how to step into those vacuums and create motion. They work hard to generate movement—the sort of movement that can transform a group into a tribe.

A student can sit in a classroom and accept what the teacher is sending out, then do the work and get by. Or she can take initiative and lead. She can provoke and question and ask for more.

A marketer can offer a product, take orders, and move on. Or he can use interactions with prospects to create something more, to surprise and delight and generate far more than just a customer who got her money's worth.

This posture of leaning in is rare and valuable. In the spring of 2008, I announced a paid summer internship for students. More than 130 well-educated students from all over the world applied. As an experiment, I set up a private Facebook group for the applicants and invited each one to participate. Sixty of them joined immediately.

No tribe existed yet—just sixty strangers in an online forum.

Within hours, a few had taken the lead, posting topics, starting discussions, leaning in and leading. They called on their peers to contribute and participate.

And the rest? They lurked. They sat and they watched. They were hiding, afraid of something that wasn't likely to happen.

Whom would you hire?

How could the lurkers imagine that doing nothing would increase the chances that they'd be selected? Were they hoping that they'd meet someone interesting or discover something new by just watching?

The experiment was perfect in that there were no externalities, no side discussions, no special cases—just sixty or so people, each demonstrating behavior that came naturally.

Not all leadership involves getting in the face of the tribe. It takes just as much effort to successfully get out of the way. Jimmy Wales leads Wikipedia not by inciting, but by enabling others to fill the vacuum. My leadership of the internship application process involved setting the stage and stepping back, not pushing at every step along the way.

The one path that never works is the most common one: doing nothing at all.

Nothing at all feels safe and it takes very little effort. It involves a lot of rationalization and a bit of hiding as well.

The difference between backing off and doing nothing may appear subtle, but it's not. A leader who backs off is making a commitment to the power of the tribe, and is alert to the right moment to step back in. Someone who is doing nothing is merely hiding.

Leadership is a choice. It's the choice to not do nothing.

Lean in, back off, but don't do nothing.

Participating Isn't Leading

Twenty percent of the population of Canada now uses Facebook. Many of those users have the false impression that joining a group somehow matters. It doesn't. (And Canadians aren't the only ones with the same impression.)

Sending in your résumé, showing up at the networking reception, hanging out at the singles bar—these are dumb ways to lead the tribe, and they're not even useful ways to be seen as a valued member.

Showing up isn't sufficient. Friending ten or twenty or a thousand people in Facebook might be good for your ego but it has zero to do with any useful measure of success.

Case Studies: CrossFit.com and Patientslikeme.com

CrossFit is a tribe of slightly crazy (okay, really crazy) fitness fanatics. These are people who on any given day will do a routine like this one:

> Fifteen handstand push-ups, followed by one pull-up, followed by thirteen handstand push-ups, followed by three pull-ups, followed by eleven handstand push-ups, followed by five pull-ups, followed by nine handstand push-ups, followed by seven pull-ups, followed by seven handstand push-ups, followed by nine pull-ups, followed by five handstand push-ups, followed by eleven pull-ups, followed by three handstand push-ups, followed by thirteen pull-ups, followed by one handstand push-up, followed by fifteen pull-ups

And they'll do it in a timed competition against thousands of people around the world. On the day I checked their site, more than four hundred people had posted their times on this particular workout.

There are certification courses across the country and they are invariably sold out weeks or months in advance. A growing cadre of certified trainers are opening gyms around the world, each gym finding its own new members of the CrossFit tribe, all coordinated by the central Web site.

The CrossFit tribe is strong and getting stronger. And it's largely the work of Greg Glassman, otherwise known as Coach. Coach has built the CrossFit tribe from scratch, inspiring and cajoling and laying down the rules. No Coach, no tribe.

Glassman innately understands how to lead the tribe. He pushes them to the limit every day. He creates an environment where the tribe not only *wants* to share news and ideas and camaraderie with one another, but is *able* to. And the tribe grows because individuals proudly segregate themselves and speak up on behalf of the tribe, simultaneously recruiting and hazing new members.

Compare this to patientslikeme.com, a Web site I discovered via an article in the *New York Times*.

Here's a tribe that appears to be leaderless. There are more than seven thousand ill people, each sharing all the details of his or her diagnosis and current health status. From dosages to side effects, the group is building an ever-growing database of real-world data about treatments for Parkinson's and other debilitating diseases. And they're supporting one another with enthusiasm and comfort as they go.

There is no Greg Glassman or Oprah Winfrey cheering them on. They cheer one another on—and who better, because no one can appreciate what they're going through more than they can.

But the founders of patientslikeme.com are leaders nonetheless. They found a tribe that desperately wanted to communicate, and they gave them the tools to do so. They made the tribe tighter. That's leadership as well.

Leaning in or backing off, but not doing nothing.

Three Hungry Men and a Tribe

When you get a chance, head over to http://msg150.com. This blog is obsessively chronicling every restaurant in a sixteen-block square of Seattle. For each restaurant (most of them are Asian), they include details like the length of the chopsticks and the contents of the bonus fortune cookie.

Here's a quote:

I was looking forward to this place, cause some Amazon buddies rated it quite highly. It's a small place, requiring us to eat in the neighboring food court (which is awesome, cause I like hanging out with crack addicts). As is typical I ordered typical fare, menu item number 1, the Tonkatsu. It advertised that it contained "slice of pork," which just wasn't going to work for me. I opted for extra pork.

. . . This ramen is like a bowl of fatty pork in butter with some noodles added for texture. I admire their bravery in serving this to me. It should come with a carton of Newports, for clearly my health is not their concern. The broth, though

flavorful, is overwhelmed with the fatness of the pork.
However, the pork is fantastic, delicious, and cooked to the
point where it falls apart.

I don't know about you, but I want in. I want to eat at every
one of these restaurants, I want to post my own reviews, I want
to join this tribe. If they ask me to pitch in, I will. I'm in.

Others will scoff and move on, wondering what the obsession is all about. That's what makes it a tribe, of course. There
are insiders and outsiders.

Curiosity

A fundamentalist is a person who considers whether a fact is
acceptable to his religion before he explores it.

As opposed to a curious person who explores first and then
considers whether or not he wants to accept the ramifications.

A curious person embraces the tension between his religion and something new, wrestles with it and through it, and
then decides whether to embrace the new idea or reject it.

Curious is the key word. It has nothing to do with income,
nothing to do with education, and certainly nothing to do
with organized religion. It has to do with a desire to understand, a desire to try, a desire to push whatever envelope
is interesting. Leaders are curious because they can't wait to

find out what the group is going to do next. The changes in the tribe are what are interesting, and curiosity drives them.

Curious people count. Not because there are a lot of them, but because they're the ones who talk to people who are in a stupor. They're the ones who lead the masses in the middle who are stuck. The masses in the middle have brainwashed themselves into thinking it's safe to do nothing, which the curious can't abide.

It's easy to underestimate how difficult it is for someone to become curious. For seven, ten, or even fifteen years of school, you are required to not be curious. Over and over and over again, the curious are punished.

I don't think it's a matter of saying a magic word; *boom* and then suddenly something happens and you're curious. It's more about a five- or ten- or fifteen-year process where you start finding your voice, and finally you begin to realize that the safest thing you can do feels risky and the riskiest thing you can do is play it safe.

Once recognized, the quiet yet persistent voice of curiosity doesn't go away. Ever. And perhaps it's such curiosity that will lead us to distinguish our own greatness from the mediocrity that stares us in the face.

What we're seeing is that fundamentalism really has nothing to do with religion and everything to do with an outlook, regardless what your religion is.

The Plurality Myth

In order to win an election, you need more than half the votes. Ideally, more than half of the population will support you, but you win if you get more than half the voters.

In order to lead a tribe, no such rule applies. All you need to do is motivate people who choose to follow you. The rest of the population is free to ignore you or disagree with you or move on.

Starbucks doesn't serve coffee to the majority of people in the United States. The New York City Crochet Guild appeals to just a small percentage of the people who encounter it. That's okay. You don't need a plurality or even a majority. In fact, in nearly every case, trying to lead everyone results in leading no one in particular.

This leads to an interesting thought: you get to choose the tribe you will lead.

Through your actions as a leader, you attract a tribe that wants to follow you. That tribe has a worldview that matches the message you're sending.

If you are leading a tribe focused on saving the world by fighting global warming, the tribe will, of course, have a worldview that includes the idea that global warming is a problem and that it can be addressed through its actions. They come to the tribe with that in mind and your leadership resonates with them.

If, on the other hand, you choose to work to persuade a different group, one with a very different worldview, they will likely reject you. Al Gore started leading his tribe when he didn't know who they were. He stated his message and people found him.

Ultimately, people are most easily led where they wanted to go all along. While that may seem as if it limits your originality or influence, it's true. Fox News didn't persuade millions of people to become conservatives; they just assembled the tribe and led them where they were already headed.

The Schoolteacher Experiment

Imagine two classrooms with similar teachers. One has fifteen students, the other, thirty-two. Which group gets a better education?

All other things being equal, the smaller class will always do better. The teacher has more time to spend customizing the lesson to each student. She has fewer students, hence fewer disruptions as well.

Now, flip the experiment around. What if the fifteen students are begrudgingly taking the course as a requirement for graduation, while the thirty-two had to apply to be admitted and are excited to be there.

No contest.

Tribes are increasingly voluntary. No one is forced to work for your firm or attend your services. People have a choice of which music to listen to and which movies to watch.

So great leaders don't try to please everyone. Great leaders don't water down their message in order to make the tribe a bit bigger. Instead, they realize that a motivated, connected tribe in the midst of a movement is far more powerful than a larger group could ever be.

The Virtuous Cycle Versus the Exclusive Tribe

Some businesses get better when they get bigger. Some non-profits do as well. Tribes that work better when they're bigger get bigger.

Political parties, for example, thrive when they're the majority. Facebook works precisely because everyone uses it. You have a fax machine only because everyone you work with does too.

But bigger isn't always the answer.

Some tribes do better when they're smaller. More exclusive. Harder to get into. Some tribes thrive precisely because they're small. Push to make one of these tribes bigger and you might just ruin the entire thing. "No one goes there anymore; it's too popular."

It's always a choice. Your choice.

Most People Don't Matter So Much

Most people like the products they already have, so marketers ignore them.

Most people work hard to fit in, so others don't notice them.

Most people like eating at places where they've eaten before.

Most people think this book is a bad idea.

Most people would like the world to stay just as it is, but calmer.

Most people are afraid.

Most people didn't use Google until last year.

Most people aren't curious.

You're not most people.

You're not the target market for most marketers, and you're certainly not a manager.

Not only aren't leaders most people, but the members of the most important tribes aren't most people either.

You're not going to be able to grow your career or your business or feed the tribe by going after *most people*. Most people are really good at ignoring new trends or great employees or big ideas.

You can worry about most people all day, but I promise you that they're not worried about you. They can't hear you, regardless of how hard you yell.

Almost all the growth that's available to you exists when you aren't like most people and when you work hard to appeal to folks who aren't most people.

Does the Status Quo Ruin Your Day (Every Day)?

How was your day?

Are you stuck with the way things were, instead of busy turning things into what they could be?

Heretics have a plan. They understand that changing the status quo is not only profitable, but fun too.

Being a heretic, an outsider, and a rabble-rouser feels scary. Why bother?

They Burn Heretics at the Stake

They also drown them, denounce them, ignore them, and hang them from the rafters.

I should have used the past tense. None of that is true anymore. Now, we invite heretics to Davos. Heretics get elected to Congress. Heretics make a fortune when their companies go public. Heretics not only love their jobs; they get a private jet too.

The image of the stake is hard to forget. It touches us in a way that's almost primal. But it's also obsolete. Marketing has made sure of that. The same forces that taught us to drink Coke for breakfast or spend $800 on a handbag are now at work on the status quo.

Heretics are too numerous to burn at the stake. So we celebrate them.

The Wrong Question

We're almost there, but some of you are itching to ask me exactly the wrong questions, which are:

"How do I do this?" Or even worse:

"How do I get my boss to let me do this?"

Or to be really blunt:

"What's the risk-free way to insinuate myself into the system so I get approval to make change?"

Surely, there's a method of making change without being burned at the stake?

It turns out that there is, but you already know what it is. Belief.

Nobody is going to listen to your idea for change, sagely shake his head, and say, "Sure, go do that."

No one anoints you as leader.

Nobody is going to see your PowerPoint presentation and hand you a check.

Change isn't made by asking permission. Change is made by asking forgiveness, later.

All You Need to Know Is Two Things

The first thing you need to know is that individuals have far more power than ever before in history. One person can change an industry. One person can declare war. One person can reinvent science or politics or technology.

The second thing you need to know is that the only thing holding you back from becoming the kind of person who changes things is this: lack of faith. Faith that you can do it. Faith that it's worth doing. Faith that failure won't destroy you.

Our culture works hard to prevent change. We have long had systems and organizations and standards designed to dissuade people from challenging the status quo. We enforce our systems and call whoever is crazy enough to challenge them a heretic. And society enforces the standards by burning its heretics at the stake, either literally or figuratively.

But the world has changed a lot. There are heretics everywhere you look. It's so asymmetrical that burning heretics isn't particularly effective any longer. As a result, more and more people—good people, people on a mission, people with ideas that matter—are stepping forward and making a difference.

Just about every system, whether it's political, financial, or even religious, has become asymmetrical. The process has turned upside down: scale isn't the same as power; in fact, scale can hurt. We've seen this in the war in Iraq as much as we've seen it in the war in the soda aisle or in the growth of new religions. In each case, an individual or a small group has the power to turn an existing system on its head.

Now, most of the time, we call heretics leaders.

The heretics are winning. You can (and must) join them.

The Balloon Factory and the Unicorn

I'm not sure you've ever visited a balloon factory. Probably not.

The people who work in the balloon factory are timid. Afraid, even. They're very concerned about pins, needles, and porcupines. They don't like sudden changes in temperature. Sharp objects are a problem as well.

The balloon factory isn't really a bad place to work if you rationalize a bit. It's steady work, with a bit of a rush around New Year's. The rest of the time it's quiet and peaceful and not so scary.

Except when the unicorns show up.

At first, the balloon factory folks shush the unicorn and warn him away. That often works. But sometimes, the unicorn ignores them and wanders into the factory anyway.

That's when everyone runs for cover.

It's amazingly easy for a unicorn to completely disrupt a balloon factory. That's because the factory is organized around a single idea, the idea of soft, quiet stability. The unicorn changes all that.

The balloon factory is all about the status quo. And leaders change the status quo.

Leaders Are Generous

In today's supercharged political (and TV) environment, it's easy to believe that in order to lead, you need to be an egomaniac, a driven superstar intent on self-glorification and aggrandizement.

In fact, the opposite is nearly always the case.

Leaders who set out to give are more productive than leaders who seek to get. Even more surprising is the fact that the intent of the leader matters. The tribes can sniff out why someone is asking for their attention. Looking out for number one is an attitude, and it's one that doesn't pay.

So we have CEOs who sit in cubicles, just like everyone else. We find successful religious leaders who don't fly by private jet or have a limo waiting for them outside. We watch eighty-four-year-old former president Jimmy Carter building houses for the poor. The benefits to these leaders aren't monetary or based on status . . . instead, they get their compensation from watching the tribe thrive.

As the ability to lead a tribe becomes open to more people, it's interesting to note that those who take that opportunity (and those who succeed most often) are doing it because of what they can do for the tribe, not because of what the tribe can do for them.

Don't Forget the Big Mac and the Microwave Oven

In 1967, just outside of Pittsburgh, a third-tier McDonald's franchisee named Jim Delligatti broke the rules and invented a new sandwich. Within a year, the Big Mac was on the menu of McDonald's restaurants around the world. (They even serve a meatless version in India.)

Jim wasn't focused on managing his franchise at the expense of everything else. Instead, he became a leader. Not blessed with a title or official sanction, Jim led the entire corporation in a new direction.

In 1946, Percy Spencer, a low-ranking engineer at the Raytheon Corporation, was trying to improve radar technology when he accidentally melted a chocolate candy bar. Being pretty smart, Percy realized that he had invented the microwave oven. (Next step: microwave popcorn.) Within decades, the microwave oven was a must-have appliance in almost every American home.

The remarkable thing about these two stories is how rare they are. We keep hearing about the invention of Post-it notes and other apocryphal tales, precisely because there aren't that many to choose from. For a long time, if you wanted to get something done, you started at the top or you got really lucky. Leverage came from cash and organizational commitment. If Bill Gates or Jack Welch or Lyndon Johnson thought something was a good idea, it was much more likely to get done.

Welcome to the age of leverage. Bottom-up is a really bad way to think about it because there is no bottom. In an era of grassroots change, the top of the pyramid is too far away from where the action is to make much of a difference. It takes too long and it lacks impact. The top isn't the top anymore because the streets are where the action is.

The new leverage available to everyone means that the status quo is more threatened than ever, and each employee now has the responsibility to change the rules before someone else does.

This isn't about working your way up to the top by following the rules and *then* starting down the path of changing your world. Instead, these innovations are examples of leadership, about one heretic, someone with a vision who understood the leverage available, who went ahead and changed things.

A few industries do fine by embracing the status quo. The list is getting shorter every day, though. If you ship oil around the world or sell credit cards or want to get elected village supervisor, you can probably coast for a while longer, embracing the old rules. But not that much longer. It seems that every factory is under pressure: every balloon maker not only fears the unicorn but desperately needs one.

Kellogg's owns hundreds of millions of dollars' worth of cereal factories. They have a well-trained sales force, miles of shelf space, and tons of advertising. So why was Bear Naked able to build a significant business right under their nose? Without expensive factories or a huge sales force, Bear Naked took a very simple, very traditional product and changed the way many people buy their breakfast.

Bear Naked didn't try to manage a portfolio of assets. They didn't try to protect the factory (they didn't have one to protect). Instead, they led the way down a different path, one based on fashion and change and leverage.

Odds are that growth and success are now inextricably linked to breaking the old rules and setting your organization's new rules loose in an industry too afraid to change.

Climbing Rocks

Chris Sharma is a heretic who climbs rocks.

Chris changed the rules of an entire sport and, along the way, influenced the way tens of thousands of people think about personal achievement.

For hundreds of years, rock climbers followed a simple principle: one foot and one hand on the wall at all times. If you're anchored with two out of your four limbs, you can do a pretty good Spiderman imitation without risking your life. Right left right left, up you go, little risk, plenty of progress.

Instead of staying glued to the wall, Chris jumps.

It's called a dyno. Chris didn't invent the dyno, but he certainly pushed it further than anyone ever expected it could go. Chris can climb routes that were previously deemed impossible. When he gets to a dead end, he looks up and jumps. No legs, no arms. Just air. Straight up, two or three or four feet, grabbing a small clump of rock with two fingers, and continuing his climb.

For a while, this was controversial. It wasn't right. It was *risky*. And then, bit by bit, the guys in the factory came around. They discovered that it was a reasonable (but surprising) solution to a large number of rock-climbing problems. Suddenly, impossible routes weren't impossible any longer.

The guess is, because Chris fits the stereotype of the typical heretic, you're not convinced. He's a loner; he's risking his life and doing absolutely absurd things forty feet over the Mediterranean (and landing on his back in the water on a regular basis). It's easy to look at Chris and say, "I could never do that." And you'd be right. You and I will never dyno a 5.14a rock arch.

The lesson isn't that you need to risk your fingers (not to mention your life) on a rock. The lesson is that one person with a persistent vision can make change happen, whether climbing rocks or delivering services.

Here's a simple way to think about it: Obe Carrion, former U.S. rock-climbing champion, won a tournament in an unusual way. Obe was one of four finalists, and each had to climb a very difficult route up a steep wall. The first three finalists did the same thing. They entered the roped-off area, inspected the route, and then slowly began climbing, one hold at a time, working their way up to the top. Two made it (with a slip or two); one fell.

Obe was scheduled to go last. He came out of the isolation area, inspected the route, took twenty steps back and he *ran* up the wall. He didn't hesitate or interpolate or hedge his bets. He just committed.

It turns out that this was the easiest way up the wall. Leaning into the problem made the problem go away.

Who Settles?

Settling is no fun. It's a malignant habit, a slippery slope that takes you to mediocrity. Managers settle all the time. They don't really have a choice because there are too many competing priorities.

Heretics don't settle. They're not good at that. Managers who are stuck, who compromise to keep things quiet, who battle the bureaucracy every day—they're the ones who settle. What else can they do?

The art of leadership is understanding what you can't compromise on.

Fear, Faith, and Religion

People who challenge and then change the status quo do something that's quite difficult. They overcome the resistance of people they trust, people they work for, people in their community. Every step along the way, it's far easier to stop and accept the thanks of the balloon factory workers for finally giving up than it is to persist and risk the humiliation of failure.

So why do it?

Faith is the unstated component in the work of a leader and I think faith is underrated.

Paradoxically, religion is vastly overrated.

Faith goes back a long way. Faith leads to hope, and it overcomes fear. Faith gave our ancestors the resilience they needed to deal with the mysteries of the (pre-science) world. Faith is the dividing line between humans and most other species. We have faith that the sun will rise tomorrow, faith that Newton's laws will continue to govern the way a ball travels, and faith that our time in med school will pay off twenty years from now because society is still going to need doctors.

Chris Sharma is able to do a dyno on a rock face one hundred feet above ground because he has faith that it'll work out okay. If you watch kids learning how to dyno, you'll see that the secret to developing the skill isn't about building their muscles or learning some exotic technique. It is merely about developing the faith that it'll work. "Merely," of course, is a huge step. It's nothing but a few neurons' worth of faith, just the knowledge that you can do it. But without faith, the leap never works.

Faith is critical to all innovation. Without faith, it's suicidal to be a leader, to act like a heretic.

Religion, on the other hand, represents a strict set of rules that our fellow humans have overlaid on top of our faith. Religion supports the status quo and encourages us to fit in, not to stand out.

There are countless religions in our lives, not just the capital-R religions like Zoroastrianism or Judaism. There's the IBM religion of the 1960s, for example, which included workplace protocols, dress codes, and even a precise method for presenting ideas (on an overhead projector). There's the religion of Broadway, which determines what a musical is supposed to look and feel like. There's the religion of the MBA, right down to the standard curriculum and perceptions of what is successful (a job at Bain & Company) and what's sort of flaky (going to work for a brewery).

Religion Works Great When It Amplifies Faith

That's why human beings invented religion. It's why we have spiritual religions and cultural religions and corporate religions. Religion gives our faith a little support when it needs it, and it makes it easy for your peers to encourage you to embrace your faith.

Religion at its best is a sort of mantra, a subtle but consistent reminder that belief is okay, and that faith is the way to get where you're going.

The reason we need to talk about this, though, is that often religion does just the opposite. Religion at its worst reinforces the status quo, often at the expense of our faith. They had a religion at Woolworth's department store, and sticking, without variation, to the principles that made the store great prevented them from turning it into a new, better kind of experience. The store is long gone, of course.

They have a religion at the country club down the street as well. A set of convictions and rules that is just too hard to change. As a result, an entire generation of professional women won't join that club, and it's going to fade and blow away soon.

Challenge Religion and People Wonder if You're Challenging Their Faith

The reason it's so difficult to have a considered conversation about religion is that people feel threatened. Not by the implied criticism of the rituals or irrationality of a particular religious practice, but because it feels like criticism of their faith.

Faith, as we've seen, is the cornerstone that keeps our organizations together. Faith is the cornerstone of humanity; we can't live without it. But religion is very different from faith. Religion is just a set of invented protocols, rules to live by (for now). Heretics challenge a given religion, but do it from a very strong foundation of faith. In order to lead, you must challenge the status quo of the religion you're living under.

Of course, religion and faith go together. You can remind yourself of your faith by wearing the company uniform or uttering the mantra of your current religion. You can embrace the support of the community by showing up at church or at the company picnic and following the rituals of whichever religion is being practiced. Without religion, it's easier for faith to flag. It's no wonder that religion has been around forever. It reinforces faith, and we can't succeed without it.

So successful heretics create their own religions. *Fast Company* magazine was a new testament for a new religion. It brought together a new group of friends, new supporters, new rituals. The same thing happens at companies that embrace heretical behavior (like IDEO) and at blogs or even at Buck's restaurant in Silicon Valley or the TED conference or other places where leaders like to hang out. These religions exist for one reason—to reinforce our faith.

You can do this on purpose. You can recognize the need for faith in your idea, you can find the tribe you need to support you, and yes, you can create a new religion around your faith. Steve Jobs did it on purpose at Apple and Phil Knight is famous for doing it at Nike.

Switching Religions Without Giving Up Faith

A recent study by the Pew Research Center for the People and the Press found that about a third of all Americans have left the religion they grew up with. The study mistakenly uses the word *faith*, but in fact, few of these people have lost faith. What they've done instead is change the system they use for reinforcing that faith.

When you fall in love with the system, you lose the ability to grow.

Faith Is What You Do

If religion comprises rules you follow, faith is demonstrated by the actions you take.

When you lead without compensation, when you sacrifice without guarantees, when you take risks because you believe, then you are demonstrating your faith in the tribe and its mission.

Of course it's difficult. But leaders will tell you that it's worth it.

A Word for It

Religion and faith are often confused. Someone who opposes faith is called an atheist and widely reviled. But we don't have a common word for someone who opposes a particular religion.

Heretic will have to do.

If faith is the foundation of a belief system, then religion is the façade and the landscaping. It's easy to get caught up in the foibles of a corporate culture and the systems that have been built over time, but they have nothing at all to do with the faith that built the system in the first place.

Change is made by people, by leaders who are proud to be called heretics because their faith is never in question.

In the year 1515, the Council of Trent wrote this about heretics: "Finally, all the faithful are commanded not to presume to read or possess any books contrary to the prescriptions of these rules or the prohibition of this list. And if anyone should read or possess books by heretics or writings by any

author condemned and prohibited by reason of heresy or sus-
picion of false teaching, he incurs immediately the sentence of
excommunication."

Boy, are you in trouble. Better get rid of this book.

Over-the-Top Underdog Bravery

For about a decade, I've carried a coin in my gear bag. It is one
of seventy coins I gave to the team I led at Yoyodyne, a company I started. Attached to the coin is a little tag that celebrates
our group and our "Over-the-Top Underdog Bravery."

Leadership almost always involves thinking and acting like
the underdog. That's because leaders work to change things,
and the people who are winning rarely do.

What we did was (and what you do is) courageous. It requires bravery. Managing doesn't, and following the rules to
make a living doesn't. It might be hard work, but it feels safe.
Changing things—pushing the envelope and creating a future
that doesn't exist yet (at the same time you're criticized by
everyone else)—requires bravery.

And over the top? That's easy. Ordinary thinking and ordinary effort are almost never enough to generate leadership.
That's because our inclination is to do barely enough. It
takes something extraordinary, a call to action that is irresistible, and a cause worth fighting for to make people actually
join in.

If you're not over the top, you're not going to have any chance at all of making things happen.

The Easiest Thing

The easiest thing is to react.

The second easiest thing is to respond.

But the hardest thing is to initiate.

Reacting, as Zig Ziglar has said, is what your body does when you take the wrong kind of medicine. Reacting is what politicians do all the time. Reacting is intuitive and instinctive and usually dangerous. Managers react.

Responding is a much better alternative. You respond to external stimuli with thoughtful action. Organizations respond to competitive threats. Individuals respond to colleagues or to opportunities. Response is always better than reaction.

But both pale in comparison to initiative. Initiating is really and truly difficult, and that's what leaders do. They see something others are ignoring and they jump on it. They cause the events that others have to react to. They make change.

Take the Follow

The merits of leadership are so ingrained that it's natural to say, "I'll take the lead."

Sometimes, though, it may make more sense to take the follow. Leading when you don't know where to go, when you don't have the commitment or the passion, or worst of all, when you can't overcome your fear—that sort of leading is worse than none at all.

It takes guts to acknowledge that perhaps this time, right now, you can't lead. So get out of the way and take the follow instead.

The Difference Between Things That Happen to You and Things You Do

In the old model, things happened to you at work. Factories opened, people were hired. Bosses gave instructions. You got transferred. There were layoffs. You got promoted. Factories closed.

Leaders, on the other hand, don't have things happen to them. They do things.

In the middle of the mortgage crisis, I spent some time with a few thousand Realtors at their annual convention. What I discovered might surprise you. The group was completely split.

Some of the Realtors saw what the media, Bear Stearns, the banks, and the public were doing *to* them and to their hard-won careers. They were angry (even bitter) about the end of a long run of increasing housing prices, and they were scared about their futures. These Realtors didn't know how they were going to cope with what had happened. They wanted to manage their careers, but change was making it impossible.

The other Realtors were palpably excited. They were eager to get to work. They saw the change in the outside world as an opportunity, a chance for them to dramatically increase their business. They knew that the current problems wouldn't last forever, and they understood that the problems would wipe out the opportunity seekers, leaving the professionals standing. Some 10 or 20 percent of the Realtors were going to quit, and the leaders, the ones who were going to stay, realized that this change was a very good thing. The same way soldiers realize that it's war that makes generals, these brokers were ready and motivated to use change as a chance to really wreak some havoc on the status quo.

Permeability

Perhaps you work for Boeing or Monsanto or some other corporate behemoth. It's more likely, though, that you work for a small organization, perhaps as small as just a few people.

Either way, it's worth taking a minute to remind yourself of how it used to be.

It used to be that executives had secretaries who had secretaries. That you sent a memo to your boss (and only your boss) and then waited a week or a month for a response. That you didn't share a new idea with a coworker—the direction of information was preferably down, or sometimes up, then down, but never sideways.

Art Kleiner's deeply researched classic, *The Age of Heretics*, tells stories, one after another, of corporate heretics who ended up demoted, fired, disgraced, and unhappy. Corporations might as well have been run by Joseph Stalin—they had unalterable five-year plans, sharply controlled channels of communication, and a royal court surrounding the monarch. Organizations used to be managed, with no place for leaders, no use for heretics.

Growing up, I used to visit my dad's office. I still remember the sign next to the corporate office men's room: "No plant workers." Not only weren't the skilled and smart lathe operators allowed to use the men's room in the adjoining office, but they weren't often invited to share what they knew with their bosses either.

The system was rigid. Kodak, for example, literally kept its workers in the dark, toiling in a pitch-black factory as they made film. While the process required darkness, it didn't require rigid management or the hoarding of information and power. That just came with the territory.

The problem with this approach is that it doesn't respond well to a changing world. And it certainly doesn't do well when information comes in from many directions, from many sources. When everyone you worked with read the *Harvard Business Review* and the same study from McKinsey, it was easy.

Top management now wants leaders. It wants heretics who will create change before change happens to them. Top management understands that they need followers, that they have to engage the tribe with change and remarkable initiative.

But the rank and file hesitates.

We hesitate because we've seen what's happened before. We're afraid of failure, of criticism, of making a mistake, and of getting caught. We worry that we'll lose our jobs if we stop managing and start leading.

The age of leverage changes this, but the fear remains. The old stories of what happened to Joe or Bob or Sue thirty years ago are told over and over. We use them to stoke our fear, to rationalize our desire to hide.

News flash: The heretics not only live to tell about it now; they actually thrive. Jerry Shereshewsky was a heretic at Young & Rubicam, where his brash nature didn't sit well with the buttoned-down culture of a 1970s advertising agency.

No worries. Jerry went on to make a name for himself at BMG and then with me at Yoyodyne, then at Yahoo, and now at a Web start-up called grandparents.com. Quite a career. If he had kept his mouth shut, he'd still be marketing coffeemakers.

Leaders Go First

"Everyone will think it's stupid!"

"Everyone says it's impossible."

Guess what? Everyone works in the balloon factory and everyone is wrong.

The status quo is persistent and resistant. It exists because everyone wants it to. Everyone believes that what they've got is probably better than the risk and fear that come with change.

Everyone in the developing world believes that things are going to be the way they were. So when entrepreneurship and technology show up in a village in Kenya, everyone resists.

Everyone at a fading record company believes that the only way to make a living is to own the income stream from selling CDs or digital downloads. So when new business models present themselves, everyone ignores them, or worse, sues.

Everyone at Microsoft believed that the company was invincible and that the piddling search engines and Internet companies in the Valley couldn't possibly represent a threat. Steve Ballmer, CEO of Microsoft, said, "Google's not a real company. It's a house of cards." He also said, "There can't be any more deep technology in Facebook than what dozens of people could write in a couple of years. That's for sure."

Over and over, everyone is wrong—unless you believe that innovation can change things, that heretics can break the rules, and that remarkable products and services spread.

If you believe that, then you're not everyone. Then you're right.

Watching the Music Business Die

It's not as if they didn't see it coming. It took almost a decade for this thriving, hyperprofitable industry to cave in on itself. The reasons are truly simple:

1. Music industry executives didn't have the heretic they needed. No one stood up and made change happen.

2. They forgot to embrace their tribe.

Taking a look at the music business is a useful education for any heretic. It demonstrates how exceedingly intelligent people in a fairly new industry willfully ignored the world around them and hid. Those lessons apply to just about every industry you can imagine.

The first rule the music business failed to understand is that, at least at first, the new thing is rarely as good as the old thing was. If you need the alternative to be better than the status quo from the very start, you'll never begin.

Soon enough, the new thing will be better than the old thing. But if you wait until then, it's going to be too late. Feel free to wax nostalgic about the old thing, but don't fool yourself into believing that it's going to be here forever. It won't.

The second rule they missed is that past performance is no guarantee of future success.

Every single industry changes and, eventually, fades. While you may have made money doing something a certain way yesterday, there's no reason to believe you'll succeed at it tomorrow.

The music business had a spectacular run alongside the baby boomers. Starting with the Beatles and Dylan, music industry executives kept minting money. The expanded purchasing power of teens, combined with the birth of rock, the invention of the transistor, and changing social mores meant a long, long growth curve.

As a result, the music business built huge systems. They created top-heavy organizations, dedicated superstores, a loss-leader touring industry, extraordinarily high profit margins,

MTV, and more. It was a well-greased system, but the key question is: Why did it deserve to last forever?

It didn't. Yours doesn't either.

The music business was built around five pillars:

- Free radio promotion
- A limited number of competing music labels
- The high cost of production, requiring musicians to get financing from labels
- The Top 40 hits–based focus of the baby boomer generation
- A high-margin, nonreproducible medium (the LP)

Notice that none of these five pillars has anything to do with tribes or leadership.

One by one, each of these five pillars has crumbled over the past five years. The result is that while there is still plenty of music, the music business is in trouble.

The innovation: use digital distribution and the Internet like radio, but do it better. Be in the services/souvenir business, instead of suing customers and yearning for the old days. Find thousands of tribes for thousands of musicians and lead them where they want to go.

The best time to change your business model is while you still have momentum.

It's not so easy for an unknown artist to start from scratch and build a career self-publishing. Not so easy for her to find fans, one at a time, and build an audience. Very, very easy for a record label or a top artist to do so. So the time to jump was yesterday. Too late. Okay, how about today?

The sooner you do it, the more assets and momentum you have to put to work.

Don't Panic When the New Business Model Isn't as "Clean" as the Old One

It's not easy to give up the idea of manufacturing CDs with a 90 percent gross margin and switch to a blended model of concerts and souvenirs, of communities and greeting cards and special events and what feels like gimmicks.

Get over it. It's the only option if you want to stay in this business. You're not going to sell a lot of CDs in five years, are you?

If there's a business here, the first few in will find it; the rest will lose everything.

The industry willfully failed to read the writing on the wall.

Industries don't die by surprise. It's not as if you didn't know it was coming. It's not as if you didn't know whom to call (or hire).

What was missing was leadership—an individual (a heretic)

ready to describe the future and build the coalitions necessary to get there.

This isn't about having a great idea (it almost never is). The great ideas are out there, for free, on your neighborhood blog. Nope, this is about taking initiative and making things happen.

The last person to leave the current record business won't be the smartest, and he won't be the most successful either. Getting out first and staking out the new territory almost always pays off.

I know it's hard to believe, but the good old days are yet to happen, even for the music business. The thing is, the guys who ran it in the old days won't be around when it regroups, because they won't be welcome.

Sheepwalking

I define *sheepwalking* as the outcome of hiring people who have been raised to be obedient and giving them brain-dead jobs and enough fear to keep them in line.

You've probably encountered someone who is sheepwalking.

The TSA screener who forces a mom to drink from a bottle of breast milk because any other action is not in the manual. A customer service representative who will happily read aloud a company policy six or seven times but never stop to consider what the policy means. A marketing executive who buys millions of dollars' worth of TV time even though she knows it's not working—she does it because her boss told her to.

It's ironic but not surprising that in our age of increased reliance on new ideas, rapid change, and innovation, sheepwalking is actually on the rise. That's because we can no longer rely on machines to do the brain-dead stuff.

We've mechanized what we could mechanize. What's left is to cost-reduce the manual labor that must be done by a human. So we write manuals and race to the bottom in our search for the cheapest possible labor. And it's not surprising that when we go to hire that labor, we search for people who have already been trained to be sheeplike.

Training a student to be a sheep is a lot easier than the alternative. Teaching to the test, ensuring compliant behavior, and using fear as a motivator are the easiest and fastest ways to get a kid through school. So why does it surprise us that we graduate so many sheep?

And graduate school? Because the stakes are higher (opportunity, cost, tuition, and the job market), students fall back on what they've been taught: to be sheep. Well-educated sheep, of course, but compliant nonetheless.

And many organizations go out of their way to hire people who color inside the lines, who demonstrate consistency and compliance. And then these organizations give these people jobs where they are managed via fear. Which leads to sheep-walking ("I might get fired!").

The fault doesn't lie with the employee, at least not at first. And of course, the pain is often borne by both the employee and the customer.

Is it less efficient to pursue the alternative? What happens when you build an organization that's flat and open and treats employees with respect? What happens when you expect a lot and trust the people you work with? At first, it seems crazy. There's too much overhead, too little predictability, and way too much noise. This isn't the top-down model of the factory, or the king and his court. It's chaos. It's easy to reject out of hand.

Then, over and over, we see something happen. When you hire amazing people and give them freedom, they do amazing stuff. And the sheepwalkers and their bosses watch and shake their heads, certain that this is an exception and that it is way too risky for their industry or their customer base.

I was at a Google conference last month, and I spent some time in a room filled with (pretty newly minted) Google sales reps. I talked to a few of them for a while about the state of the industry. And it broke my heart to discover that they were sheepwalking.

Consider the receptionist at a publishing company I visited a week later. There she was, doing nothing. Sitting at a desk, minding her own business, bored out of her skull. She acknowledged that the front office is very slow and that she just sits there, reading romance novels and waiting. And she's been doing it for two years.

Or consider the MBA student I met yesterday who is taking a job at a major packaged-goods company because they offered her a great salary and promised her a well-known brand. She's going to stay "for just ten years, then have a baby and leave and start my own gig." She'll get really good at running coupons in the Sunday paper, but not particularly good at solving new problems.

What a waste.

Step one is to give the problem a name. Sheepwalking. Done.

Step two is for those of you who see yourself in this mirror to realize that you can always stop. You can always claim the career you deserve merely by refusing to walk down the same path as everyone else just because everyone else is already doing it.

The biggest step, though, comes from anyone who teaches or hires. And that's to embrace nonsheep behavior, to reward it and cherish it. As we've seen, just about everywhere there's been growth lately is where the good stuff happens.

(I just reread these paragraphs, and I'm betting some people will think I'm being way too harsh. That depends. It depends on whether you believe that people have a considerable amount of innate potential, that work is too time consuming to be dull, and that organizations need passion (from employ-ees and from customers) if they want to grow into tribes and movements. It depends on whether you believe that the relationship between marketers and the people they touch is important enough to invest in. I think if you believe all that, if you believe in yourself and your coworkers, then this isn't nearly harsh enough. We need to hurry. We need to wake up.)

How Was Your Day?

It's four a.m. and I can't sleep. So I'm sitting in the lobby of a hotel in Jamaica, checking my e-mail.

A couple walks by, obviously on their way to bed, having pushed the idea of vacation a little too hard. The woman looks over to me and, in a harsh whisper a little quieter than a yell, says to her friend, "Isn't that sad? That guy comes here on vacation and he's stuck checking his e-mail. He can't even enjoy his two weeks off."

I think the real question—the one they probably wouldn't want to answer—was, "Isn't it sad that we have a job where we spend two weeks avoiding the stuff we have to do fifty weeks a year?"

It took me a long time to figure out why I was so happy to be checking my e-mail in the middle of the night. It had to do with passion. Other than sleeping, there was nothing I'd rather have been doing in that moment—because I'm lucky enough to have a job where I get to make change happen. Even though I don't have many people working for me, I'm in the business of leading people, taking them somewhere we want to go.

On the other hand, most people have jobs (for now) where they fight change, where they work overtime to defend the status quo. It's exhausting. Maintaining a system in the face of change will grind you down.

Think for a second about the people you know who are engaged, satisfied, eager to get to work. Most of them, I'll bet, make change. They challenge the status quo and push something forward—something they believe in. They lead.

"Life's too short" is repeated often enough to be a cliché, but this time it's true. You don't have enough time to be both unhappy and mediocre. It's not just pointless, it's painful. Instead of wondering when your next vacation is, maybe you ought to set up a life you don't need to escape from.

The amazing thing is that not only is this sort of life easier to set up than ever before, but it's also more likely to make you successful. And happy. So how was your day?

The Thermometer and the Thermostat

A thermostat is far more valuable than a thermometer.

The thermometer reveals that something is broken. The

thermometer is an indicator, our canary in the coal mine. Thermometers tell us when we're spending too much or gaining market share or not answering the phone quickly enough. Organizations are filled with human thermometers. They can criticize or point out or just whine.

The thermostat, on the other hand, manages to change the environment in sync with the outside world. Every organization needs at least one thermostat. These are leaders who can create change in response to the outside world, and do it consistently over time.

Your Micromovement

This is the heart of the matter: every leader cares for and supports a movement. A movement like the free speech movement at Berkeley or the democracy movement in Tiananmen Square or the civil rights movement in Mississippi. Or maybe a movement like the obsession with hand-roasted coffee in Brooklyn or the worldwide collection of people obsessed with tattoos.

Today, you can have a narrow movement, a tiny movement, a movement in a silo. Your movement can be known by ten or twenty or a thousand people, people in your community or people around the world. And most often, it can be the people you work with or for, or those who work for you.

The Web connects people. That's what it does. And movements take connected people and make change.

What marketers and organizers and people who care are discovering is that they can ignite a micromovement and then be propelled by the people who choose to follow it.

The key elements in creating a micromovement consist of five things to do and six principles:

1. *Publish a manifesto.*

   Give it away and make it easy for the manifesto to spread far and wide. It doesn't have to be printed or even written. But it's a mantra and a motto and a way of looking at the world. It unites your tribe members and gives them a structure.

2. *Make it easy for your followers to connect with you.*

   It could be as simple as visiting you or e-mailing you or watching you on television. Or it could be as rich and complex as interacting with you on Facebook or joining your social network on Ning.

3. *Make it easy for your followers to connect with one another.*

   There's that little nod that one restaurant regular gives to another recognized regular. Or the shared drink in an airport lounge. Even better is the camaraderie developed by volunteers on a political campaign or insiders involved in a new product launch. Great leaders figure out how to make these interactions happen.

4. *Realize that money is not the point of a movement.*
   Money exists merely to enable it. The moment you try to cash out is the moment you stunt the growth of your movement.

5. *Track your progress.*
   Do it publicly and create pathways for your followers to contribute to that progress.

Principles:

1. *Transparency really is your only option.*
   Every failed televangelist has learned this the hard way. The people who follow you aren't stupid. You might go down in scandal or, more likely, from ennui. People can smell subterfuge from a mile away.

2. *Your movement needs to be bigger than you.*
   An author and his book, for example, don't constitute a movement. Changing the way people apply to college does.

3. *Movements that grow, thrive.*

    Every day they get better and more powerful. You'll get there soon enough. Don't mortgage today just because you're in a hurry.

4. *Movements are made most clear when compared to the status quo or to movements that work to push the other direction.*

    Movements do less well when compared to other movements with similar goals. Instead of beating them, join them.

5. *Exclude outsiders.*

    Exclusion is an extremely powerful force for loyalty and attention. Who *isn't* part of your movement matters almost as much as who is.

6. *Tearing others down is never as helpful to a movement as building your followers up.*

That Building Down the Street

I think it is a boat club, but perhaps it's a political party or even a corporate headquarters. It might even be a franchise business or a local nonprofit. All I know is that there's a tribe working overtime to maintain the status quo.

The congregation shows up every week and does the same

ritual it did last week, goes through the same motions and nothing changes. In fact, nothing changes *precisely* because of the ritual. The tribe exists, apparently, to stamp out change.

The customer service staff shows up and follows the handbook and treats every customer exactly the same and can't figure out why they're being disrespected in return.

The volunteers go through the motions of supporting the nonprofit, but they're the same motions they've always gone through and they're getting the same results they've always gotten.

Some tribes are engaged in change. Many are not. And it doesn't matter whether it's a church or a corporation, the symptoms are the same. The religion gets in the way of the faith. Static gets in the way of motion. Rules get in the way of principle.

People show up because they have to, not because they want to. Desire is defeated by fear, and the status quo calcifies, leading to the long slow death of the stalled organization.

It's so sad to watch and it's so common.

Leadership is the antidote, and it works in every building if you let it.

Every Tribe Is a Media Channel

TIME magazine is a media channel. So are CNN and Yahoo. The advantage of traditional media channels is that they're available for rent. Send in some money and buy some time. The time gets you eyeballs or possibly even attention. And that attention might lead to sales.

Google realized that every search (more than a billion a day) is a media channel as well. And they've profited by selling those channels one click at a time.

Tribes are different.

Tribes are the most effective media channels ever, but they're not for sale or for rent. Tribes don't do what you want; they do what they want. Which is why joining and leading a tribe is such a powerful marketing investment.

How to Be Wrong

John Zogby, the successful pollster, was completely, utterly wrong about Al Gore in Florida. By ten points. And he was wrong about John Kerry, and wrong about his prediction for the New Hampshire primaries in 2008. But notice that I said "successful pollster," not "disgraced pollster." If he wasn't willing to be wrong, he'd be unable to be right as often as he is.

Isaac Newton was totally, fantastically wrong about alchemy, the branch of science he spent most of his career on. He was as wrong as a scientist could be. And yet, he's widely regarded as the most successful scientist and mathematician ever.

Steve Jobs was wrong about the Apple III, wrong about the

Mac FX, wrong about the NeXT computer. Insanely wrong. You know the rest.

The secret of being wrong isn't to avoid being wrong!

The secret is being willing to be wrong.

The secret is realizing that wrong isn't fatal.

The only thing that makes people and organizations great is their willingness to be not great along the way. The desire to fail on the way to reaching a bigger goal is the untold secret of success.

I've been waiting for you to ask for the shortcut, the error-free, failure-free way to get people to do what you want, to make change happen without risk or fear, to magically alter the status quo. That, after all, is the best way to sell you on the ideas here. If I could just give you the answer, you'd be leading a tribe right now.

The honest answer is: There isn't an easy way. It isn't easy for middle managers or CEOs or heretics. The truth is that they appear to risk everything, but in fact, the risk isn't so bad. The downsides are pretty small because few of us are likely to get burned at the stake.

The secret of leadership is simple: Do what you believe in. Paint a picture of the future. Go there.

People will follow.

The Timing of Leadership

It's rare that it's obvious when to lead. Sure, there are times when you know you need to stand up, take a position, spread an idea, clear out an obstacle, and be brave.

But more often than not, great leadership happens when the tribe least expects it. The nonobvious moments are the ones that count. Like now, perhaps.

The Reactionary Tribe

So far, we've been talking about tribes as leadership-loving, fast-moving, progressive organizations that thrive on change. And most tribes, especially as they grow, are just that.

But sooner or later, tribes get stuck. Let's look at Wikipedia again. Wikipedia is a nonprofit that is run by a conservative board and several thousand dedicated volunteers. And most of them don't want anything at all to change.

In recent months, Wikipedia volunteers have gone on a campaign to delete tens of thousands of pages that don't meet the tribe's vague standards. At the same time, Florence Nibart-Devouard, the chairwoman of the Wikipedia board, is actively campaigning to ensure that no one makes particularly large donations to the foundation. She was quoted by the *New York Times* as saying that she would "make some noise" if an aggressive outsider was to try to become a board member.

What to do with a tribe like this?

If your goal is to make change, it's foolish to try to change the worldview of the majority if the majority is focused on maintaining the status quo. The opportunity is to carve out a new tribe, to find the rabble-rousers and change lovers who are seeking new leadership and run with them instead.

Yes, I think it's okay to abandon the big, established, stuck tribe. It's okay to say to them, "You're not going where I need to go, and there's no way I'm going to persuade all of you to follow me. So rather than standing here watching the opportunities fade away, I'm heading off. I'm betting some of you, the best of you, will follow me."

Possibility of Risk

I was listening to a talking head on the radio, and he was prattling on about a "probability of risk" related to some course of action in the future. People are so afraid of risk they can't even use the word. Risk, after all, is a probability of failure, right? So this guy was warning us of a probability of a probability. He couldn't even say it.

It's all a risk. Always.

That's not true, actually. The only exception: it's a certainty that there's risk. The safer you play your plans for the future, the riskier it actually is. That's because the world is certainly, definitely, and more than possibly changing.

When Tribes Replace What You're Used To

The brilliant venture capitalist Fred Wilson got me thinking about what purpose a traditional firm (corporation, nonprofit, church, whatever) serves. He quotes Ronald Coase, the Nobel laureate in economics:

> There are a number of transaction costs to using the market; the cost of obtaining a good or service via the market is actually more than just the price of the good. Other costs, including search and information costs, bargaining costs, keeping trade secrets, and policing and enforcement costs, can all potentially add to the cost of procuring something with a firm. This suggests that firms will arise when they can arrange to produce what they need internally and somehow avoid these costs.

In other words, we start formal organizations when it's cheaper than leading a tribe instead. Having employees, for example, gives you a tight interaction of communication and output that used to be difficult to accomplish from a less formal tribe. Having soldiers, for example, is seen as more reliable than earning the trust and support of the entire population.

The Internet changes this because you can build a bigger, faster, cheaper tribe than you used to be able to. The new economy changes this because the transaction costs are falling fast while the costs of formal organizations (offices, benefits, management) keep increasing.

Many big organizations are getting bigger as a way of fighting off the power of tribes. They buy other companies, hoping that the formal nature of their bigness will somehow successfully fight off the flexible, fast, and sometimes free power of the tribe. I think that's unlikely.

Initiative

The timid leave a vacuum.

Workers in the balloon factory are always afraid, particularly of something happening. Things that happen are rarely good, because they disturb the status quo.

That's why initiative is such an astonishingly successful tool: because it's rare. Even a little bit of action, a few new ideas, or a tiny bit of initiative can fill the vacuum. It's a big deal to spill just a few drops of Hawaiian Punch on a spotless white tablecloth. People notice.

When Barbara Barry, the now famous furniture designer, was looking for a manufacturing partner for her first line of sofas, she invited executives from a leading manufacturer to her showroom in Los Angeles.

Before she did that, though, she took some initiative.

First, she managed to place a wholesale order for reams of fabric that the manufacturer traditionally used on its own furniture.

She rented an office big enough to turn into a showroom.

She designed a line of furniture that was bold and even breathtaking, and then she had a local shop build one of each piece, upholstered in the company's signature fabric.

When the executives arrived, expecting a sales pitch and some drawings, they saw finished sofas. Made from their materials, with their brand label sewn on. After the fact, it's easy to say that it wasn't much—a few thousand dollars' worth of custom furniture. But in that moment, for that industry, it was more than enough. It changed the rules.

Barbara wasn't managing her career or asking permission from the furniture executives. She was leading, and enjoying every moment of it.

The organizations that need innovation the most are the ones that do the most to stop it from happening. It's a bit of a paradox, but once you see it, it's a tremendous opportunity.

Stuck on Stupid

My colleague Gil likes to quote U.S. Army Lieutenant General Russel Honoré, pointing out that too many people get "stuck on stupid."

I'm imagining that your colleagues aren't stupid. But when the world changes, the rules change. And if you insist on playing today's games by yesterday's rules, you're stuck. Stuck with a stupid strategy. Because the world changed.

Some organizations are stuck. Others move quickly. In a changing world, who's having more fun?

Mark Rovner, Nonprofit Heretic

Mark has been challenging the status quo of the nonprofit world for years. He's very successful at it and he's having a ball.

Here's one example of the sort of trouble that leaders need to cause. Mark started an online debate about the future of direct mail fund-raising. This income stream is the lifeblood of most nonprofits, and it's drying up. The Internet, of course, is supposed to be the solution to all problems, but as Mark points out, it's not.

> The era of cheap direct mail and high response rates in acquisitions is over. The economics of direct mail are failing.

That is more or less an uncontroverted fact. It costs more to mail, and fewer new donors come back with each mailing. This trend has been masked somewhat by higher average gifts by donors you already have, but sooner or later, the acquisition crisis is going to affect bottom lines. For some, it already has.

What currently passes for an online fundraising model is at best a stopgap.

My take: I despair for most of the top fifty nonprofits in the United States. These are the big guys, and they're stuck. Far more than the Fortune 100, not known for being cutting edge in themselves, the top charities rarely change. If you're big, you're used to being big and you expect to stay big. That means that generation after generation of staff has been hired to keep doing what's working. Big risks and crazy schemes are certainly frowned upon.

The good news is this: the Internet is not a replacement for direct mail fund-raising. It is, in fact, something much bigger than that for just about every nonprofit.

As soon as commerce started online, many nonprofits generated lots of income from their Web sites. This was mistakenly chalked up to brilliant conversion and smart marketing. In fact, it was the result of technologically advanced donors using a more convenient method to send in money they would have sent in anyway.

The big win is in changing the very nature of what it means

to support a charity. The idea of "I gave at the office" and of giving money in the last week in December speaks to obligation. Many people donate to satisfy a guilty feeling or to please a friend. This doesn't scale. Not one bit. It's super easy to ignore a direct mail solicitation when all you have to do is hit Delete and no one notices.

The big win is in turning donors into patrons and activists and participants. The biggest donors are the ones who not only give, but also do the work. The ones who make the soup or feed the hungry or hang the art. My mom was a volunteer for years at the Albright-Knox Art Gallery in Buffalo, New York, and there's no doubt at all that we gave more money to the museum than we would have if they'd sent us a flyer once a month.

The Internet allows some organizations to embrace long-distance involvement. It lets charities flip the funnel, not through some simple hand waving but by reorganizing around the idea of engagement online. This is the new leverage. It means opening yourself up to volunteers and encouraging them to network, to connect with one another, and, yes, even to mutiny. It means giving every one of your professionals a blog and the freedom to use it. It means mixing it up with volunteers so they have something truly at stake. This is understandably scary for many nonprofits, but I'm not so sure you have a choice.

Do you have to abandon the old ways today? Of course not. But responsible stewardship requires that you find and empower the heretics and give them the flexibility to build something new, instead of trying to force the Internet to act like direct mail with free stamps.

The Posture of a Leader

If you hear my idea but don't believe it, that's not your fault; it's mine.

If you see my new product but don't buy it, that's my failure, not yours.

If you attend my presentation and you're bored, that's my fault too.

If I fail to persuade you to implement a policy that supports my tribe, that's due to my lack of passion or skill, not your shortsightedness.

If you are a student in my class and you don't learn what I'm teaching, I've let you down.

It's really easy to insist that people read the manual. It's really easy to blame the user/student/prospect/customer for not trying hard, for being too stupid to get it, or for not caring enough to pay attention. It might even be tempting to blame those in your tribe who aren't working as hard at following as you are at leading. But none of this is helpful.

What's helpful is to realize that you have a choice when you communicate. You can design your products to be easy to use. You can write so your audience hears you. You can present in a place and in a way that guarantees that the people you want to listen will hear you. Most of all, you get to choose who will understand (and who won't).

Switching Tribes

As your tribe grows, it's tempting to accelerate that growth, to find more people to join the tribe.

The most obvious prospects, of course, are already members of other tribes. If you can persuade that rabid soccer fan to switch to football instead, it's a coup. Or consider the full-page ad in the *New York Times* paid for by hundreds of evangelical Christians, encouraging religious Jews to switch teams. And there goes a politician, eagerly courting the loudest partisans from the other side to join her team instead.

This rarely works.

People don't like to switch. We may eagerly join a company and slog through a job for years, staying until the place finally declares bankruptcy. No, it's not the same company we joined at the beginning, far from it, but to switch sides is to admit that we made a mistake.

Growth doesn't come from persuading the most loyal members of other tribes to join you. They will be the last to come around. Instead, you'll find more fertile ground among seekers, among people who desire the feeling they get when they're part of a vibrant, growing tribe, but who are still looking for that feeling.

I'm not talking about disaffected outsiders, loners who work hard not to affiliate. I'm talking about people at the fringes, individuals who might jump from one thing to another with less angst.

If you're trying to persuade the tribe at work to switch from one strategy to the other, don't start with the leader of the opposition. Begin instead with the passionate individuals who haven't been embraced by other tribes yet. As you add more and more people like these, your option becomes safer and more powerful—*then* you'll see the others join you.

Not Now, Not Yet

The largest enemy of change and leadership isn't a "no." It's a "not yet." "Not yet" is the safest, easiest way to forestall change. "Not yet" gives the status quo a chance to regroup and put off the inevitable for just a little while longer.

Change almost never fails because it's too early. It almost always fails because it's too late.

The curve below shows the benefits of almost any innovation over time:

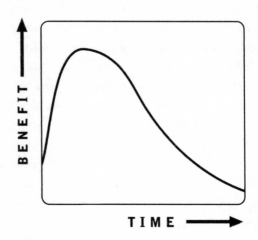

By the time you realize that your corner of the world is ready for an innovation, it's almost certainly too late. It's definitely not too early.

"It's not time," "Take it easy," "Wait and see," "It's someone else's turn"—none of these stalls are appropriate for a leader in search of change. There's a small price for being too early, but a huge penalty for being too late. The longer you wait to launch an innovation, the less your effort is worth.

Understanding the Trick

Magician and essayist Jamy Ian Swiss has written about the annoying and shortsighted kid who shouts out to the performing magician, "I know how you do that trick!"

Does it really matter that you know?

The world is jam-packed with books and manuals on how to do the trick, whatever the trick is. The leadership trick has been endlessly dissected. So if it's so easy to figure out how to do the trick, why do so few people do it? If it's so easy to figure out how to do the Twisted Aces or the French Drop, why are so few people amazing?

Because, of course, it has nothing to do with knowing how the trick is done, and everything to do with the art of doing it. The tactics of leadership are easy. The art is the diffcult part.

Adam Gopnik quotes Swiss as saying, "Magic only happens in a spectator's mind. Everything else is a distraction. . . . Methods for their own sake are a distraction. You cannot cross over into the world of magic until you put everything else aside and behind you—including your own desires and needs—and focus on bringing an experience to the audience. This is magic. Nothing else."

Substitute "leadership" for "magic" and there you are.

Leadership is very much an art, one that's accomplished only by people with authentic generosity and a visceral connection to their tribe. Learning the trick won't do you any good if you haven't made a commitment first.

The Revolution Will Not Be Televised

It seems as though we rarely get to see leadership in action. We tend to notice it after the fact or after it's gathered steam. That's because it starts where we least expect it.

In industry after industry, the market leader isn't the one who develops the innovation that turns the industry upside down. In organization after organization, real leadership rarely comes from the CEO or the senior VP of leadership. Instead, it happens out of the corner of your eye, in a place you weren't watching.

Criticizing Hope Is Easy

And in the end, cynicism is a lousy strategy.

Hope without a strategy doesn't generate leadership. Leadership comes when your hope and your optimism are matched with a concrete vision of the future and a way to get there. People won't follow you if they don't believe you can get to where you say you're going.

Managers are the cynical ones. Managers are pessimists because they've seen it before and they believe they've already done it as well as it can be done. Leaders, on the other hand, have hope. Without it, there is no future to work for.

The Naked Violinist

Tasmin Little is a violin prodigy who has managed to keep her career going long after many others have faded. As one of the great violinists working today, she has had concert tours and booking agents and a record deal.

Her new record, though, is free. It's online at http://www .tasminlittle.org.uk and you can listen to all of it, along with commentary and notes, for free.

Tasmin is leading a movement. She is investing time and energy in a committed, consistent effort to spread classical music. She didn't just upload an MP3 file. She regularly visits prisons and small towns and schools to perform. She adds value to her site in addition to the music. She's not a dilettante; she's a leader.

I have no doubt that her original idea was met with resistance or even derision. Too many sacred cows, too much status in the status quo. Even as she persisted, her initial efforts were unlikely to have met with universal acclaim, with worldwide publicity and huge applause. Only her focus and drive and commitment made it work.

Writing Songs That Spread

My friend Jacqueline tells the story of how Unicef spent a fortune creating posters to promote the idea of child vaccination to the mothers of Rwanda. "The posters were gorgeous—photographs with women and children with simple messages written in Kinyarwandan (the local language), about the importance of vaccinating every child. They were perfect, except for the fact with a female illiteracy rate exceeding 70 percent, words written in perfect Kinyarwandan made little difference."

Jacqueline noticed that the way messages spread in Rwanda was by song. One group of women would sing a song for other women, both as a way of spreading ideas and as a gift. No song, no message.

Your tribe communicates. They probably don't do it the way you would; they don't do it as efficiently as you might like, but they communicate. The challenge for the leader is to help your tribe sing, whatever form that song takes.

The X Prize

Peter Diamandis wanted to energize the tribe of inventors, financiers, and explorers who might pursue new solutions for space flight. Rather than blindly following the limited leadership that NASA provided, he decided to offer the X Prize, a $10 million award for the first team that could put a rocket one hundred kilometers into space successfully, twice in two weeks.

The team that won spent more than $20 million to collect the prize. All told, a simple act of leadership generated an investment by the dozens of teams that competed that was greater than ten times more than the prize itself. But more important, it generated a brand-new field, with new participants and a new sort of community.

Peter told me that when he first broached the idea, everyone thought it was stupid. He had no instant support, no one applauding or eager to sign up at first blush. It was his leadership and commitment that made it occur, not the idea itself (which was nothing but an update of the prize that Lindbergh won more than half a century earlier). The idea wasn't the point. Organizing the tribe was.

Who Cares?

Caring is the key emotion at the center of the tribe. Tribe members care what happens, to their goals and to one another. Many organizations are unable to answer the question "Who cares?" because in fact, no one really does. No one really cares if the menu changes or if the percentage of fundraising income used for overhead changes. No one really cares if the widget's color is changed or if the flight is staffed with a different crew.

If no one cares, then you have no tribe. If you don't care—really and deeply care—then you can't possibly lead.

The Elements of Leadership

Leaders challenge the status quo.

Leaders create a culture around their goal and involve others in that culture.

Leaders have an extraordinary amount of curiosity about the world they're trying to change.

Leaders use charisma (in a variety of forms) to attract and motivate followers.

Leaders communicate their vision of the future.

Leaders commit to a vision and make decisions based on that commitment.

Leaders connect their followers to one another.

Sorry for the alliteration, but that's the way it worked out.

If you consider the leaders in your organization or community, you'll see that every one of them uses some combination of these seven elements. You don't have to be in charge or powerful or pretty or connected to be a leader. You do have to be committed.

Understanding Charisma

Think about the charismatic leaders you've encountered. They might be young or old, rich or poor, black or white, male or female, extroverted or shy. In fact, the only thing they seem to have in common is that they are leaders.

I think most people have it upside down. Being charismatic doesn't make you a leader. Being a leader makes you charismatic.

There are leaders with speech impediments and a fear of public speaking. Leaders way down the corporate ladder and leaders with no money or obvious trappings of power. There are ugly leaders too, so charisma certainly isn't about being attractive.

It's easy to give in to your fear and tell yourself that you don't have what it takes to lead. Mostly, people give up when they get to the charisma part of the checklist. "I wasn't born charismatic, not like those other guys, so I guess I'll just settle for following."

The flaw in this reasoning is that those other guys weren't born charismatic either. It's a choice, not a gift.

Ronald Reagan's Secret

What most people want in a leader is something that's very difficult to find: we want someone who listens.

Why is it so hard to find a leader who can listen?

Because it's easy to confuse listening to individuals with "going with the crowd" or "following the polls." It's easy for a leader with a vision to give up on listening because, after all, most people want you to be average, and that doesn't get you anywhere. If Henry Ford had listened, the old saying goes, we'd have better buggy whips today, not cars.

The secret, Reagan's secret, is to listen, to value what you hear, and then to make a decision even if it contradicts the very people you are listening to. Reagan impressed his advisers, his adversaries, and his voters by actively listening. People want to be sure you heard what they said—they're less focused on whether or not you *do* what they said.

When Graham Weston, executive chairman of Rackspace, wanted to persuade his talented and somewhat skittish staff to move with him to the new headquarters in a depressed area of town, he didn't lecture them or even try to cajole them. All he did was listen. He met with every one of the employees who was hesitating about the move and let them air their views. That's what it took to lead them: he listened.

Listen, really listen. Then decide and move on.

The Forces of Mediocrity

Maybe it should be "the forces *for* mediocrity."

There's a myth that all you need to do is outline your vision and prove it's right—then, quite suddenly, people will line up and support you.

In fact, the opposite is true. Remarkable visions and genuine insight are always met with resistance. And when you start to make progress, your efforts are met with even more resistance. Products, services, career paths—whatever it is, the forces for mediocrity will align to stop you, forgiving no errors and never backing down until it's over.

If it were any other way, it would be easy. And if it were any other way, everyone would do it and your work would ultimately be devalued. The yin and yang are clear: without people pushing against your quest to do something worth talking about, it's unlikely to be worth the journey. Persist.

How to Sell a Book (or Any New Idea)

My friend Fred has a new book coming out and he was trolling around for marketing ideas. I think he'd be surprised at this one: Sell *one*.

Find one person who trusts you and sell him a copy. Does he love it? Is he excited about it? Excited enough to tell ten friends because it helps them, not because it helps you?

Tribes grow when people recruit other people. That's how ideas spread as well. The tribe doesn't do it for you, of course. They do it for each other. Leadership is the art of giving people a platform for spreading ideas that work. If Fred's book spreads, then he's off to a great start. If it doesn't, he needs a new book or a better platform.

Hard Just Got Easy

. . . and vice versa.

It used to be really hard to plow the field, really hard to find the steel needed to build a car, and really hard to get a package from New York to Cleveland on time for a reasonable price.

It used to be really hard to get a new company funded and really hard to get shelf space so consumers could find your product. It used to be really hard to run a factory.

Those things are easy now. They might cost more than we'd like, but you can put them on a checklist and they'll get done.

What's hard now is breaking the rules. What's hard is finding the faith to become a heretic, to seek out an innovation and then, in the face of huge amounts of resistance, to lead a team and to push the innovation out the door into the world.

Successful people are the ones who are good at this.

When the Los Angeles Philharmonic, one of the most prestigious in the world, went looking for a new conductor, they had their pick of perhaps a thousand qualified individuals. These were world-class people who had been tested and proved at doing the work of running an orchestra the traditional way.

They hired Gustavo Dudamel.

He is a twenty-six-year-old sensation from Venezuela whose résumé can't compare to those of his elder peers. He doesn't have the proven abilities at doing yesterday's hard work. The Los Angeles Philharmonic realized, though, that they could always find someone to get that work done. What they needed was a leader to bring the organization to a new audience in a new way.

Stop for a second and consider the implications of this decision. From a thousand qualified conductors (who understood the status quo), the Philharmonic chose a newbie who wanted to challenge it. Heretics discover this sort of success all the time.

Which Would You Prefer: Trial or Error?

It's a myth that change happens overnight, that right answers succeed in the marketplace right away, or that big ideas happen in a flash.

They don't. It's always (almost always, anyway) a matter of accretion. Drip, drip, drip. Improvements happen a bit at a time, not as grand-slam home runs that are easy to get.

Four million iPhones later (that's more than a billion dollars in less than a year), it's easy to forget that pundit Laura

Reis said the Apple phone would never succeed. Visa and MasterCard were huge ideas that took years to take off. Even little things, like that restaurant with a line out the door—it didn't open that way.

If your organization requires success before commitment, it will never have either.

Part of leadership (a big part of it, actually) is the ability to stick with the dream for a long time. Long enough that the critics realize that you're going to get there one way or another . . . so they follow.

Positive Deviants

How do you manage leaders?

Given that leaders can appear anywhere in an organization, it seems to me that the job of senior management is to find them and support them. Leaders have tribes of their own, and someone needs to lead those tribes.

Which leads to the idea of positive deviance.

As a general rule, managers don't like deviants. By definition, deviance from established standards is a failure for a manager working to deliver on spec. So, most of the time, most managers work hard to stamp out deviance (and the deviants who create it).

Managers stamp out deviants. That's what they do.

Leaders understand a different calculus. Leaders understand that change is not only omnipresent, but the key to success.

And it turns out that employees who are committed to change and engaged in making things happen are happier and more productive.

Putting these two facts together, it's not hard to come to the conclusion that you desperately need more leaders, more deviants—more agents of change, not fewer.

Great leaders embrace deviants by searching for them and catching them doing something right.

This is the life's work of Jerry Sternin.

Sternin went to Vietnam to try to help starving children. Rather than importing tactics that he knew would work, or outside techniques that he was sure could make a difference, he sought out the few families who weren't starving, the few moms who weren't just getting by but were thriving. And then he made it easy for these mothers to share their insights with the rest of the group.

This seems obvious, but it's heretical. The idea that an aid worker would go to a village in trouble and not try to stamp out nonstandard behavior is crazy.

"The traditional model for social and organizational change doesn't work," he told *Fast Company*. "It never has. You can't bring permanent solutions in from outside."

Leveraging the work of Marian Zeitlin, Sternin and his wife Monique have taken this approach around the world, from developing countries to hospitals in Connecticut.

Over and over again, the Sternins have discovered a simple process: find leaders (the heretics who are doing things differently and making change), and then amplify their work, give them a platform, and help them find followers—and things get better. They always get better.

I hope that's not so simple that it gets ignored, because it's important. It's such an effective idea that it saves children's lives every day. All the Sternins did was find the mom with the healthy kids. And then they helped the others in the village notice what she was doing. They gave that mom a spotlight, encouraging her to keep it up and, more important, encouraging others to follow her lead.

It's simple, but it works. It might be the most important practical idea in this entire book.

The Obligation

Not too far from us, a few blocks away, there are kids without enough to eat and without parents who care. A little farther away, hours by plane, are people unable to reach their goals because they live in a community that just doesn't have the infrastructure to support them. A bit farther away are people being brutally persecuted by their governments. And the world is filled with people who can't go to high school, never mind college, and who certainly can't spend their time focused on whether or not they get a good parking space at work.

And so, the obligation: don't settle.

To have all these advantages, all this momentum, all these opportunities and then settle for mediocre and then defend the status quo and then worry about corporate politics—what a waste.

Flynn Berry wrote that you should never use the word "opportunity." It's not an opportunity, it's an obligation.

I don't think we have any choice. I think we have an obligation to change the rules, to raise the bar, to play a different game, and to play it better than anyone has any right to believe is possible.

Where Credit Is Due

I'm frequently asked about getting credit. People want to know how to be sure they get credit for an idea, especially when they have a boss who wants to steal it. Or they want to know how to be sure to give me credit for an idea in a book or blog post of their own.

Real leaders don't care.

If it's about your mission, about spreading the faith, about seeing something happen, not only do you not care about credit, you actually *want* other people to take credit.

If you want to program your Web site with the cutting-edge tool called Ruby on Rails, feel free. The software is freely available. And you don't have to credit the guys at 37 Signals who developed it. You can just use it.

That's fine with them, because they're not trying to get credit or earn a living from the programming language. Enough people know it was their work; enough people seek them out and respect them for the work they've done. The more the language spreads, the farther the movement they started goes. And that's the real goal.

There's no record of Martin Luther King, Jr., or Gandhi whining about credit. Credit isn't the point. Change is.

The Big Yes

Rene Hromek wrote to me about the BIG YES. (The capital letters are part of the deal.) Let's contrast the BIG YES with the "little no."

The little no is easy to find and hard to avoid. The little no feels safe. It's like swatting a gnat. The little no avoids a distraction, keeps you away from a possible hassle. There are tons of little no's everywhere we look.

The BIG YES, on the other hand, is about leadership and

apparent risk. Mostly, it's about leverage. Today, more than ever, the BIG YES is available to every person lucky enough take it.

Imagination

Albert Einstein said, "Imagination is more important than knowledge." Leaders create things that didn't exist before. They do this by giving the tribe a vision of something that could happen, but hasn't (yet).

You can't manage without knowledge. You can't lead without imagination.

Fierce Protection

When Matt Groening was making *The Simpsons Movie*, the studio heads relentlessly pushed him to include paid product placements in it—more than had been in any movie ever before. The execs explained that while the extreme product placement would be insanely profitable, it would also be seen as a joke. The audience, apparently, would think it hysterically funny that the studio profited by jamming in as many placements as possible.

If Matt hadn't dug in his heels and resisted, the movie would have been ruined. Compromise may expedite a project, but compromise can kill it as well.

Belief

People don't believe what you tell them.

They rarely believe what you show them.

They often believe what their friends tell them.

They always believe what they tell themselves.

What leaders do: they give people stories they can tell themselves. Stories about the future and about change.

Why Not You, Why Not Now?

The barriers to leadership have fallen. There are tribes everywhere, many in search of leaders. Which creates a dilemma for you: without a barrier, why not begin?

Simple example: ten years ago, if you wanted to publish a book, you needed to find a publisher that would say yes. No publisher, no book.

Today, of course, you can publish a book all by yourself. Just visit Lulu.com and you're done.

Without someone to say yes, all that's left are unpublished writers who tell themselves no.

Leadership is now like that. No one gives you permission or approval or a permit to lead. You can just do it. The only one who can say no is you.

Let's continue for a minute, then, and think about when.

Do you have what you need to lead? Do you need more power or education or money? When will you have enough of what you need in order to start leading a tribe?

If someone gave you two weeks to give that speech or write that manifesto or make that decision, would that be enough time? If two weeks aren't enough, are four or twelve or a thousand?

In my experience, leaders don't need to wait. There's no correlation between money, power, or education and successful leadership. None. John McCain was fifth in his class (from the bottom) at the United States Naval Academy. Howard Schultz sold kitchen gadgets and ended up at an underfunded three-store coffee bean chain before he turned it into Starbucks. Gandhi was a lawyer in South Africa. Waiting doesn't pay. Saying yes does.

The Perfect Fallacy

Quality is not only not necessary, for many items it's undesirable.

If we define quality as regularly meeting the measured specifications for an item, then quality matters a lot for something like a pacemaker. It doesn't matter at all for a $3,000 haute couture dress.

More fashion = less need for quality.

Perfect is an illusion, one that was created to maintain the status quo. The Six Sigma charade is largely about hiding from change, because change is never perfect. Change means reinvention, and until something is reinvented, we have no idea what the spec is.

Yahoo and the Peanut Butter Memo

Brad Garlinghouse probably saved Yahoo (for a while, anyway). Either way, he found his tribe.

In 2006, Brad acted like a heretic. He wrote a pointed memo to his bosses at Yahoo, outlining what he saw as flaws in the company strategy, upending the company religion and describing a vision for the future. The purpose of the memo was to incite a tiny tribe, the group that ran his company with him.

The memo got leaked.

It was featured in the *Wall Street Journal* and reprinted across the Web. Suddenly, Brad was no longer just a little-known but important senior manager at Yahoo. He was every wannabe heretic's nightmare. He was in trouble.

The guys in the balloon factory hold up moments like that as warnings to the unicorn. "Be careful," they say, "or you'll get into trouble."

The thing is, Brad's memo started a chain of events that

led to CEO Terry Semel's departure and to big changes at Yahoo. It also led to an even bigger job for Brad.

What Do You Have to Lose?

Brad didn't leak the memo, but he did have the chutzpah to share a very honest appraisal with his bosses. If Brad had gotten fired, there were dozens of other (yes, I'm willing to say *better*) companies that would have given him the opportunity to work with them instead. The worst that would have happened is that he would have ended up with a better job. If the memo had worked (which it did), he would have had a better place to work and have done the right thing, not just for the shareholders but for his career.

After gaining credibility, paying his dues, doing the work, and earning trust, Brad had absolutely nothing to lose by writing that memo. It was hard, no doubt about it, but it was worth it.

What are you waiting for?

Case Study: No Kill

Nathan Winograd has no authority, he's not in charge of anything, and he can't make people do what he wants.

And yet, shelter by shelter, town by town, Nathan is

changing the way millions of dogs and cats are treated. Not by fiat or by legislation, but by leading the tribe.

Every year, about five million healthy dogs and cats are destroyed (killed) by shelters in the United States. In some shelters, the number is as high as 90 percent of all the animals handled. Nathan can't abide this, and many people agree with him. Yet the conventional wisdom (and the established tribe) made it clear that there's no way to get all those pets adopted, especially the older, uncute pets. Where would they all go? The tribe in power saw no alternative.

Starting with one shelter in one city, Winograd's mentor, Richard Avanzino, led them. He showed them that it *could* be done, and that the status quo didn't have to stay the way it was.

Avanzino implemented programs that seem like common sense but were, at the time, controversial. The San Francisco SPCA started spaying and neutering animals before adoption. They set up a foster home program (many dogs entered foster care and never came back). He even filled a van with pets and hit the road, looking for families willing to take a pet.

When Avanzino presented his results to other shelters at a conference, some attendees got up and walked out. They represented the status quo, and this tribe wasn't ready to change.

The next step is extraordinary: Avanzino took the San Francisco SPCA out of the business of capturing and killing pets, he walked away from a huge city contract, and he encouraged any staff members who didn't share his vision to get out and find a new job instead. He grew a new tribe, found new people with a new attitude, and led them.

Within a few years, his nascent organization had a surplus of millions of dollars. From this base, Avanzino tried to pass a law in San Francisco requiring the city pound to transfer all its healthy animals to the SPCA instead of killing them. What happened next is astonishing but true: major humane and vegetarian organizations came to the hearings to argue *against* the law. They said it was impossible. They said that if people thought their pets would be adopted instead of killed, they'd be more likely to abandon them (!).

So how did Avanzino get the law passed? How did his efforts to save tens of thousands of small animals succeed? Simple. His new tribe did it. The public did it. Avanzino found a group (a large group) that wanted to hear his story, that wanted to follow, that wanted to take action. By 1995, San Francisco was a No Kill city. Every healthy pet was adopted, not killed.

The story continues with Winograd. After Avanzino left San Francisco, the SPCA started to lose its nerve. Leadership flagged. They cancelled their free neutering program and started to compromise their values. Disgusted, Winograd left.

He ended up at the Tompkins County SPCA in rural New York State. Basically, he was the dog catcher, with a small budget (one that was in debt), a run-down facility, and a staff who represented the old way of doing things.

Winograd followed many of the steps you've read about in this book. He didn't compromise. The very first day on the job, he refused to kill (not euthanize or put down or put to sleep, but kill) the animals under his care. He was clear and vivid in talking with his staff and within months, half of them (the ones who didn't want to join the tribe) had left.

Nathan Winograd understood that without followers, there is no leadership. So he went directly to his public. To people who wanted to hear his story. To citizens who wanted to follow. In one year, more than four hundred media stories were written about his shelter. Donations poured in. Volunteers showed up (two hundred volunteers providing twelve thousand hours of work). In an industry where 10 or 20 percent of the animals involved are adopted, Tompkins regularly adopted out more than 85 percent, with only very sick or aggressive animals not making it.

And it wasn't a fluke. Winograd did it again in Charlottesville, Virginia. Then, after establishing a tribe, he moved to Reno, Nevada, and did it one more time. Each time with no real budget and no real power. Just with leadership.

When people hear this story, something clicks. First, the outrage that behind our backs millions of dogs and cats are killed as a matter of course. Second, the pride that one person on a mission could make such a huge difference. And third, the realization that if Nathan Winograd can change a horrible century-old tradition from the bottom up, we can too.

There are tribes out there, just waiting to be coalesced and led. All they need is a dedicated leader eager to do the right thing.

I was moved by Nathan's story. Moved by the way he pushed himself to make a difference for animals that had no chance to speak up against the status quo. Moved by his ability to see the future and make it real. And most of all, moved by his ability to mobilize a tribe and to do it in a way in which every person involved came out ahead.

The Look of the Leader

What does a leader look like?

I've met leaders all over the world, on several continents, and in every profession. I've met young leaders and old ones, leaders with big tribes and tiny ones.

I can tell you this: leaders have nothing in common.

They don't share gender or income level or geography. There's no gene, no schooling, no parentage, no profession. In other words, leaders aren't born. I'm sure of it.

Actually, they do have one thing in common. Every tribe leader I've ever met shares one thing: the decision to lead.

What, Exactly, Should You Do Now?

You made it to the end. And it's possible you missed the checklists, the detailed how-to lists, and the *For Dummies–*style instruction manual that shows you exactly what to do to find a tribe and lead it.

I think that was the point.

I can tell you that I'm going to get a lot of flak from most people about what you've just read. People might say that it's too disorganized or not practical enough or that I require you to do too much work to actually accomplish anything. That's okay. In fact, criticism like that almost always accompanies change.

Every tribe is different. Every leader is different. The very nature of leadership is that you're not doing what's been done before. If you were, you'd be following, not leading.

All I can hope for is that you'll make a choice. Every leader I've ever met has made the choice, and they've been glad they did.

You can choose to lead, or not. You can choose to have faith, or not. You can choose to contribute to the tribe, or not.

Are there thousands of reasons why you, of all people, aren't the right one to lead? Why you don't have the resources or the authority or the genes or the momentum to lead? Probably. So what? You still get to make the choice.

Once you choose to lead, you'll be under huge pressure to reconsider your choice, to compromise, to dumb it down, or to give up. Of course you will. That's the world's job: to get you to be quiet and follow. The status quo is the status quo for a reason.

But once you choose to lead, you'll also discover that it's not so difficult. That the options available to you seem really clear, and that yes, in fact, you can get from here to there.

Go.

One Last Thing

May I ask you a favor?

If you got anything out of this book, if you highlighted or circled or Post-it-ed, I'm hoping you'll do something for me:

Give this copy to someone else.

Ask them to read it. Beg them to make a choice about leadership.

We need them. We need you.

Spread the word.

Thanks.

"I'm not sure where I'm going. I'll lead!"

—EMMANUELLE HEYMAN

Acknowledgments and the Story of *Tribes*

I'm a huge fan of Cory Doctorow's. His books are terrific (not to mention the blog). A few years ago, I read *Eastern Standard Tribe*, and the idea of tribes started to stick with me.

Late in 2007, Corey Brown (no relation), the COO of Squidoo.com, a company I founded, started talking to me about tribes as well. He was pushing the idea of making it easy for Squidoo lensmasters to find and coordinate their tribes online.

Years ago, Hugh MacLeod (no relation), the world's most popular inspirational business cartoonist (who knew you could do that for a living?), drew a cartoon (his most popular one ever) with the caption, "The market for something to believe in is infinite"—as soon as I read it, I knew I wanted to write a book about that idea.

In January 2008, in speaking and writing about the music industry, I first started blogging about tribes. Six weeks later,

Kevin Kelly, the founding editor of *Wired*, wrote a post he called True Fans, which I reference here. He captured some critical thoughts about tribes and their power.

Robert Scoble, the unstoppable blogger, has interviewed numerous tribe leaders, giving me all sorts of fodder but without realizing that this is what he's been doing.

Kudos to Clay Shirky for writing *Here Comes Everybody*, which will quickly bring you up to speed on online tribes.

At the end of February 2008, I was lucky enough to read Adam Gopnik's great *New Yorker* piece about the long-lived worldwide tribe of magicians. Jamy Ian Swiss embodies, in some ways, the leadership I'm talking about.

And then, a few weeks later, in March, as I finished writing this book, my editor pointed out *Tribal Leadership*, by Dave Logan, John King, and Halee Fischer-Wright. It has a terrific title. I just went out and bought a copy, and while it has very little overlap with this book, I recommend that you read it if you get a chance.

I've had the privilege of working with the self-managing tribe of 250,000 people at Squidoo, led by Megan, Corey, Gil, Anne, Kimberly, Anne, and Blake. Thanks, guys, for showing me how it works.

There are heroes in my life, people who teach me, through their actions, not words. Jacqueline Novogratz goes to work every day and changes the world for the better. She leads a tribe that is better for her input and enthusiasm and love. She sets an example of what leadership really is. I aspire to be just a little bit like her. And my dad, Bill Godin, tirelessly works to enrich his community with the powerful work he contributes every day. He sends a message to me (and to the rest of us) through his work.

I'd also like to thank the entire skiing Heyman clan for their patience and inspiration, Megan Casey for pushing me to be remarkable, and Lisa, Will, Adrian, Mark, Courtney, and Allison for keeping their promises. Lynn Gordon, of course. Lisa Gansky too. And thanks to Catherine E. Oliver for not missing a thing.

As always, this one is for Helene. I'm glad I'm in her tribe.